JESUS AND JUDAS

American Academy of Religion
Academy Series

edited by
Susan Thistlethwaite

Number 72
JESUS AND JUDAS
Biblical Exegesis in Barth

by
Paul McGlasson

Paul McGlasson

JESUS AND JUDAS
Biblical Exegesis in Barth

Scholars Press
Atlanta, Georgia

JESUS AND JUDAS
Biblical Exegesis in Barth

by
Paul McGlasson

© 1991
The American Academy of Religion

Library of Congress Cataloging in Publication Data

McGlasson, Paul
    Jesus and Judas : biblical exegesis in Barth / Paul McGlasson.
    p. cm. — (American Academy of Religion academy series ; no.
72)
    Includes bibliographical references.
    ISBN 1-55540-567-3 (alk. paper). — (ISBN 1-55540-568-1 (pbk. :
alk. paper)
    1. Bible—Criticism, interpretation, etc. 2. Barth, Karl,
1886-1968. Kirchliche Dogmatik. I. Title. II. Series.
BS476.M335 1990   90-23560
220.6'092—dc20   CIP

Printed in the United States of America
on acid-free paper

Preface

The reader will find in the Bibliography a record of my debt to various works which, while not necessarily cited in the present study, yet form the deep background for the viewpoint and interests that were brought to it. I remember with deep gratitude Professor Hans Frei, the advisor to this dissertation; his kindness and sheer intellectual curiosity broke down all defenses. Special thanks also goes to Professor Brevard Childs for his excellent contribution to the preparation of this study. I would like to thank also Professor David Kelsey, and Professor George Lindbeck for their helpful response to my initial ideas; and Charleen Cox, who skillfully prepared the manuscript for publication. I owe a special debt of gratitude to Peggy, for her treasured friendship and support.

Table of Contents

INTRODUCTION

The *Church Dogmatics* of Karl Barth is a vast three-way conversation. The dominant voice in the conversation is of course Barth's dogmatic exposition in the main body of the text. Less voluminous, but no less insistent, are the two supportive voices, physically distinguished from the dogmatic exposition by their presence in numerous small print excursuses. These supportive voices are Barth's analysis of the history of theology and doctrine, and Barth's biblical exegesis. What follows is a study of the biblical exegesis contained in the numerous excursuses of volumes I and II of the *Church Dogmatics.*

The present study is for the most part descriptive and analytical. The aim is insight into the biblical exegesis of these volumes as a means of strengthening and deepening our knowledge of Barth's contribution to the movement of theology in the modern period.

The study deliberately focuses on the biblical exegesis of these volumes rather than the hermeneutics. Since Barth's death, of course, the question of hermeneutics has emerged as one of the key topics of contemporary theological discourse. Barth's voice has for the most part gone unheard in the more recent debate, no doubt in part due to the lack of a systematic treatment of hermeneutical problems on his part. Barth does make numerous hermeneutical comments in the course of his doctrine of Scripture in volume I.2 of the *Church Dogmatics.* Nevertheless, the questions are treated sporadically, and the problems that are handled are generated by the intramural concerns of Barth's theological explication; they are not, therefore, easily converted into the practiced and disciplined world of contemporary theological hermeneutics. The fact is, the best way to come to grips with Barth's possible contribution to contemporary theological hermeneutics is to focus on his actual biblical exegesis, rather than the less clear contours of his few hermeneutical statements. And that is the aim of the present work.

I have not, however, attempted to convert Barth's exegesis into a hermeneutical system. That is, I have attempted an analysis of the biblical exegesis as exegesis and not as the embodiment or manifestation of an underlying hermeneutic. The reason for this is simply that it corresponds with what I consider an important part of Barth's contribution to the contemporary debate: namely, the logical and material priority of biblical exegesis over hermeneutics. Thus, converting the biblical exegesis into an implied hermeneutic would lessen the impact of Barth's approach at precisely its strongest point, its strongest concern: that hearing the biblical text rightly is far more important than the condition of the possibility of that hearing. I have indeed presented the biblical exegesis in such a way that it addresses the concerns, or at least some of them, of contemporary theological hermeneutics; I have nevertheless done so while yet presenting and analyzing the exegesis as exegesis.

A disciplined and widely shared language for the description and analysis of biblical exegesis that is *not* basically a systematic hermeneutic of one sort or another is not now available. At an earlier time in theology (e.g. 16th century Protestant theology) basic exegetical rules could perform this function. No such earlier set of exegetical rules, however, is adequate to the task of describing and analyzing Barth's biblical exegesis, nor indeed can they, or should they, be substituted for the current task of articulating a better language. I have thus, for the purposes of this study, constructed a descriptive and analytical language in piecemeal fashion, whose primary purpose is at the same time accuracy in respect to Barth's exegesis and insight in respect to the contemporary debate in hermeneutics and exegesis. The language does not depend on any one system of hermeneutics, though it makes use of elements from several.

The study treats comprehensively the biblical exegesis contained in volumes I and II of the *Church Dogmatics*. I have chosen the biblical exegesis of the *Church Dogmatics* for study rather than the earlier exegesis (e.g. the *Romans* commentary) both because it is less well known and because it is, in my judgement, the more mature and lasting corpus of biblical exegesis that Barth produced. I have restricted the study to the first two volumes simply because of the exigencies of space and time. The inclusion of the biblical exegesis from the remaining volumes of the *Church Dogmatics* would not fundamentally alter the basic shape of the description and analysis here presented; it would largely consist, rather, in the multiplication of examples for study. What can and should be said about the biblical exegesis of the *Church Dogmatics* as a whole can equally well be said in an analysis of the biblical exegesis in volumes I and II (that is, of course, I.I and I.2, II.1 and II.2). Restriction of the study to these volumes simply brings more control and manageability to the presentation.

Turning now to the secondary literature on the topic of Barth's biblical exegesis, it comes as rather a surprise that there is in fact no scholarly tradition for such a study. Standard treatments of Barth's work as a whole mention the exegesis, if at all, only as an illustration of some theological point in the construal of Barth's theology.[1] And there is not a large-scale work devoted to Barth's biblical exegesis. Why is this? Why is there such a curious lack of attention to what is, after all, a sizeable fraction of Barth's mature theological production: the biblical exegesis in the *Church Dogmatics*? Whatever the ultimate explanation, one important factor is surely something like the following. Barth's biblical exegesis quite simply falls between two stools. On the one hand, professional theologians more recently have not for the most part concerned themselves professionally with technical, extended, exegetical production. And on the other hand, professional biblical scholars have not concerned themselves with an exegetical production that falls entirely outside the normative exegetical approach in modern times. The result is that, for scholars of theology, the work is too "biblical," while for scholars of the Bible the work is too "theological." The resulting fate of Barth's biblical exegesis is in a way not really surprising. At least part of Barth's reason for doing extended biblical exegesis in the context of Christian theology was to wage a direct assault on the bifurcation of scholarly work into two such separated disciplines. Theology, for Barth, should again be biblical in a technical, disciplined sense, and likewise should study of the Bible be disciplined by confessional theological concerns. The immediate result of this assault on the bifurcation of theological disciplines was that at least this part of Barth's work simply attracted no scholarly attention.

_____

[1]See, for example, the works by Balthasar, Berkouwer, Kung, and Hartwell in the Bibliography.

For the most part, the only exception to this rule has been a series of studies that, if not directly devoted to the biblical exegesis, are at least more than remotely connected to it. This is a literature which, over the years, has pursued one aspect of Barth's work: the relationship of Barth's approach to the Bible to that of historical criticism.[2] This literature is not about Barth's exegesis as such. It is rather an attempt to juxtapose a systematic reading of Barth's scattered hermeneutical comments with the author's conception of the "historical" exegesis of the Bible. Actual exegesis is mentioned, if at all, only by way of illustration of this juxtaposition.

The most illuminating example of this secondary literature is the article of Rudolf Smend entitled "Nachkritische Schriftauslegung."[3] The title, indeed, sounds the major note of the study; Barth represents, according to Smend, the post-critical, as opposed to a pre-critical, critical, or non-critical reading of the Bible. Smend argues that Barth respects the role of historical criticism of the Bible in the Church's life. Criticism of the Bible has the function of radicalizing the question of faith; therefore, theological exegesis must of necessity pass through the straightforwardly critical phase: it cannot remain pre-critical, or faith is lost. But it recognizes that *the Bible itself* because of its kerygmatic character, presses exegesis on to a wholistic, synthetic, positively theological reading of the text. The movement from criticism to post-criticism is thus an unbroken extension of the historical reading of the text. "De Wettes legitimer Nachfolger als theologischer Exeget ist nicht Wellhausen gewesen, sondern Karl Barth" (p. 225).

---

[2]See the works of Eichholz, Lindemann, Marquandt, and Smend in the Bibliography.

[3]in *Parrhesia* (Zurich: EVZ-Verlag, 1966), pp. 215-237.

Whether or not Smend's positive assessment of the relation of Barth's hermeneutic to historical criticism is accurate I am not prepared to judge. There is first of all the problem that Barth's hermeneutical comments must be systematically related together in order to make such a judgement; and this procedure is such as to give the impression that Barth had a "view" about his relation to historical criticism, which is largely untrue. But more importantly, there is the problem of determining just what "historical-criticism" is. Smend's construal is only one of many; and it does not, therefore, seem particularly useful to *interpret* Barth by measuring him against such an unstable standard.

But again, whatever one decides about the accuracy of Smend's construal and assessment, the fact remains that his study does not concern Barth's biblical exegesis at all. Barth's actual exegesis is simply not dealt with; and given the hundreds of pages of exegesis, as opposed to the occasional hermeneutical remarks, it seems rather a shaky procedure to seize on the latter as the key to interpreting the former. What Smend says about Barth's hermeneutics may or may not be true; it is certain, however, that it is uninformative in predicting and interpreting the details of Barth's biblical exegesis.

Another exception to the general rule of neglect in the study of Barth's biblical exegesis is the work of David Ford. In his book *Barth and God's Story* Ford has offered a very impressive construal of Barth's theology as a whole.[4] While it is beyond the scope of the present work to delve into the comprehensive interpretation of Barth's theology, suffice it to say that Ford offers an interpretation of Barth as a *narrative theologian*, an interpretation which has the merit of presenting a basically unified, discussable rendering of

---

[4](Frankfurt am Main: Peter Lang, 1981).

Barth's theology as a whole. It likewise has the merit of integrating a great deal of attention to the biblical exegesis into the construal of Barth's theology. Ford has also published an essay devoted to "Barth's Interpretation of the Bible."[5]

As mentioned above, Ford's general construal of Barth's theology is likewise accompanied by a general construal of Barth's biblical exegesis. Ford offers a consistent narrative interpretation. According to Ford, Barth seizes on biblical narrative as the key to the interpretation of the Bible as a whole. And Barth gives to this biblical narrative an exegesis that is formally parallel to the literary criticism of realistic narrative. In his essay (p. 77), Ford gives a general summary of the characteristic features of realistic narrative reading shared by certain types of literary criticism as well as by Barth's exegetical approach to biblical texts: "Barth, as I have shown, recognized that it is chiefly through stories that the Bible conveys its understanding of reality. He went further in insisting that this way of rendering reality is one in which form and content are inseparable. The portrayal of complexity, individuality, and particularity as they unfold in a sequence of characters and events in interaction is not something that can be understood except by following the sequence attentively. The meaning is built up cumulatively and in an irreducibly temporal form, and amounts to a rich reality to which abstractions and generalizations cannot do full justice. This way of writing is what I mean by "realistic," and it is found in many novels and biblical narratives which render a world of meaning in terms of its characters and particularities, presenting it as they go along." Barth shares this way of reading texts with many literary critics according to

---

[5]in S. W. Sykes, *Karl Barth: Studies of His Theological Method* (Oxford: Oxford University Press, 1979), pp. 55-87.

Ford; and indeed, the imaginative appreciation of realistic narrative functions as a new substitute in Barth for the rejected natural theology. Literary reading of biblical texts is a prelude to faith.[6] Finally, Ford argues that the narrative of the story of Jesus in the gospels is the narrative center for the Bible as a whole. Other narratives gain their meaning through typological association with this one central narrative; the story of Jesus has replaced the narrative line from Creation to Consummation as the meaning-structure for the Bible as a whole.

Now, Ford's proposal has the enormous advantage of offering a unified view of Barth's biblical exegesis as a whole. Using the concept of realistic narrative reading, together with the well-known Christological focus of Barth's theology, Ford is able to give a manageable, coherent perspective on an extraordinarily diffuse body of material. Furthermore, there is no doubt that something like the narrative reading of texts is a prominent feature of Barth's biblical exegesis. For these reasons, the present study owes much to Ford's ground-breaking work.

Nevertheless, Ford's research has, in my judgement, gone astray in certain unfortunate directions. Firstly, Ford ascribes to Barth an economy of method that simply isn't there. As I shall endeavor to show throughout the present work, Barth's exegesis is ultimately and irreducibly *pluralistic* methodologically; a single category like narrative reading does not begin to comprehend and explain the enormous variety that one notices immediately upon reading the biblical exegesis in any volume of the *Church Dogmatics*. Secondly, *if* one had to choose a single, explanatory interpretation of Barth, *conceptual analysis* would probably be a more likely candidate. Thirdly, Ford

---

[6]see p. 66 in "Barth's Interpretation of the Bible".

ascribes to Barth a *unified view of narrative* that isn't there; not only is narrative reading not the single comprehensive form of Barth's biblical exegesis, there is likewise nothing approaching a unified, coherent concept or method of narrative reading itself. Of course, each of these objections to Ford's work can only be argued fully in the course of the actual study below. What follows in the present work is a presentation and analysis of the biblical exegesis in *Church Dogmatics* I and II. The argument of the study is largely descriptive in nature. That is, the study will have succeeded if the exposition and analysis yield genuine insight into this much neglected aspect of Barth's work.

The procedure of the present work is as follows. Each of the four chapters to follow is formally divided into two parts. The first part contains a summary and analysis of one major aspect of Barth's biblical exegesis. The presentation in this part of the chapter is intended to apply to, and illuminate, as much of the exegesis as possible. Numerous examples are used for the purpose of rendering concrete the turns of argument in the description. The second part of each chapter contains a close analysis of only one exegetical excursus. The purpose of the analysis in this half of the chapter is the intensive understanding of the one excursus under consideration, but in such a way as to shed light on the general aspect under consideration in the chapter as a whole. The close analysis in the second half of the chapter is *not* just an illustration of the general principles introduced in the first half; the close analysis rather stands on its own as an informative contribution to the understanding of Barth's biblical exegesis. Nevertheless, the close analysis in the second half of each chapter is written in such a way as to sharpen the summary perspective presented in the first half. (Chapter 1 is an anomaly, in that the summary presentation and the close analysis are each further divided into two, so that there are four parts to the chapter.)

Each of the four chapters takes up a general aspect of Barth's biblical exegesis. Using the concept of "witness," Chapter 1 offers a construal of the general aim of Barth's biblical exegesis. The excursus studied in Chapter 1 comes from Barth's doctrine of the election of the individual, and contains material from a variety of Old Testament texts (the patriarchal narratives, Lev. 14 and 16, David and Saul, and I Kings 13). Chapter 2 isolates for study the Christological form and focus of Barth's biblical exegesis. The excursus for close analysis is Barth's exegesis of the story of the Rich Young Ruler in the gospels. Chapter 3 isolates for consideration the influence of Barth's theological concerns on his biblical exegesis, as well as his appropriation of traditional Christian theological language and the application to the study of one biblical text his understanding of another (the case of "parallel passages"). The text for close analysis in this chapter is an excursus on New Testament texts referring to the life-content of the elect. Finally, Chapter 4 attempts a general construal of Barth's methodological approach to the text of Scripture under the concept of "explication." The chapter concludes with a study of Barth's interpretation of the figure of Judas in the New Testament.

CHAPTER I

The Bible as Witness

"The Bible is a witness to the Word of God." This statement is as close as one can come to a comprehensive description of Barth's biblical exegesis. Barth repeatedly seeks throughout the Bible, and finds in it, a witness to the Word of God. "Witness" (German: *Zeugnis*) is of course Barth's word for the ecclesial-theological function of the Bible; it appears as the leading concept in the doctrine of Scripture, and is one of the most frequently used words in the *Church Dogmatics*. Nevertheless, the concept of witness is never given a full analysis by Barth; this surprising fact is perhaps explained by Barth's view that the content of hermeneutical concepts and rules is entirely parasitic upon, and can only be filled out by, actual exegesis. The Bible is witness; it is known to be such only as it is exegeted as such.

I shall here use the concept of witness to organize the study of a broad variety of features of Barth's exegesis. Two aspects of the concept of witness will provide the structure for the two sections of this chapter; the two aspects are also among the few hermeneutical comments Barth does make about witness in I.2 of the

Church   Dogmatics (pp. 457-72).   Witness, firstly,
implies a limitation: because the Bible is a witness to
the Word of God, it is not *per se* revelation itself.   It is
a human, linguistic, literary attestation of _revelation.   It
is a sacred writing.   It is written Scripture.   It is a text.
How does Barth expound the Bible as a text?   What does
the Bible look like as a text from the point of view of
Barth's exegesis of it?   Upon what features of its
textuality does he concentrate?   Which features, if any,
does he leave out?   These, and other topics, will be
discussed in section 1.

Secondly, however, the Bible as a witness to the
Word of God is truly *related* to revelation.   It really
does bear witness to it, and in so doing shares in it.   But
how?   How does the text of Scripture come to be truly
related to revelation?   In what does this relation
consist?   The answer of Barth's exegesis is *analogical
depiction*;   the biblical text depicts revelation
analogically.   In the second section of this chapter,
attention will be given to just how this takes place in
Barth's exegesis.   How does Barth expound a biblical text
as an analogical depiction of the Word of God?   This and
related questions will be the theme of the second
section.

One further comment is in order at this point.   The
concept of witness clearly has a polemical context for
Barth which, though not of direct interest to this study,
does provide some clarification for its pervasiveness in
Barth's exegesis.   The opposite of reading the Bible as
witness is reading the Bible as *expression*, an
expression of the humanity of its human authors.   To find
in it a witness is to look where it points (*hinweisen*) to
hear its content (*Sache*) as it describes an object
(*Gegenstand*).   To read it as an expression is to relate
its words and content to the human experience or
subjectivity (however conceived) of its composers--an

act, says Barth, of "shameless violence" to the integrity
of the written word of the Bible, as to any human word
desirous of communicating a message (*C.D.*, pp. 464-5;
K.D., pp. 513-15). It is clear, though unspoken in this
context in the *Church Dogmatics*, that Schleiermacher is
Barth's perceived opponent here, and Schleiermacher as
the first in a line of phenomenological hermeneutics in
theology. Certain kinds of historical criticism are no
doubt intended as well, though Barth would probably
relate the error of historical criticism to the theoretical
support it receives from Schleiermacher's type of
hermeneutics. At any rate, with this polemical context
for the concept of witness in mind, we turn now to
Barth's exegesis of the Bible as a text bearing witness
to revelation.

The Witness as Text

The biblical exegesis in the *Church Dogmatics* is,
above all, an attempt to stay close to the biblical text.
It is a remarkably sober, painstaking, almost mundane
corpus of exegesis, at least insofar as it stretches the
scope of a biblical text seemingly beyond its limits only
after the most careful and precise mapping of its
textual, literary, and theological coordinates. Evidence
for the nearly mesmerizing presence of the biblical text
in Barth's exegesis is the sheer volume of direct
quotation and citation. Ranging from the simplest
citation, to a catena of fully quoted verses in Greek or
German, to repeated allusions or references within a full
exegetical excursus, the mere text of the Bible has the
kind of immediate presence in the pages of Barth's
theology that reminds one of the literary forms of
patristic theology. At any rate, while not yet exegesis
proper, quotation of a biblical text re-emerges in
Barth's exegesis as a working component of theological
argument. One must say re-emerges: patristic,

medieval, reformation, and protestant scholastic theologies accepted the validity of the so-called proof-text; I can here only wonder whether Barth found a way to adapt and follow in a modern, or post-modern, context the kinds of rules for the use of proof texts employed in an earlier age.[1]

Barth usually presents an exegesis of the Greek or German New Testament, only the German Old Testament. He pays attention to text-critical issues; he rejects, for example, the spurious version of I John 5.7 ff. as evidence for New Testament teaching (I.1, p. 313). He likewise rejects the longer ending of the Gospel according to Mark, on the grounds that its assignment of a healing function to the post-resurrection apostolic community betrays a later ages confusion over the precise role of healing in the attestation of the messiahship of Jesus (II.2, p. 448).

It is almost without exception the final form of the biblical text that receives Barth's exegesis. While the fuller problem of Barth's relation to historical-critical exegesis will be dealt with more at length in chapter 4 below, it must here be argued that Barth knew of, and rejected, the many possibilities for reading a historically reconstructed text. Positive evidence for these assertions are the hundreds and hundreds of pages of exegesis of biblical texts as they stand in any pew Bible, texts whose surface meaning is a source of admiring attention rather that medieval (allegorical), modern (historical-critical), or post-modern impatience. Negative evidence for these same assertions are the many places in which Barth conjures up, only to reject, the reading of a historically reconstructed text. The two "parts" of Psalm 19 are one witness, not two, regardless of the prehistory of the material (II.1, pp. 101-2). Again, the Holiness Code (the very name evinces Barth's

---

[1]The history of the "proof-text" has, to my knowledge, yet to be written.

knowledge of historical criticism) has a plain unmistakable meaning only when read in the context of the Book of Leviticus and the rest of the Pentateuch (II.1, pp. 364-5). Or finally, on the possibility of reading the traditions about Saul and the traditions about David in the Old Testament in any way independently of one another: "Even if the traditions about both characters may at one time have existed separately, the meaning of both was properly understood when they were interwoven and worked in the whole in our present texts" (II.2, p. 372). I do not here suggest that Barth had no use for a historical approach to the Bible--he considered his own method preeminently historical--nor that he globally rejected the modern institution of historical criticism. At present I wish only to point out what seems obvious and trivial at first glance, and yet becomes rather more interesting and surprising as it is pondered: that Barth devoted thousands of pages to exegeting what might be called the "familiar" form of the text, as opposed to its professionally reconstructed form whether in its medieval, modern, or post-modern embodiment.

Rather surprisingly in light of the few hermeneutical rules he offers, Barth does often make an appeal to something like authorial intention. Yet the appeal is never accompanied by the attempt historically or phenomenologically to locate and determine the intention of the author. On the other hand, appeal to authorial intention is clearly not just a cypher for exegetical emphasis ("Paul really does mean this here," or the like). It is used to make exegetical choices between differing readings of a passage. Though it is frequently an appeal to a person ("Paul means," "At the back of Paul's mind"), it can also be a reference to the intentionality of a text ("the Bible would never say," "The New Testament clearly intends to suggest") or of an unknown person or persons ("the redactors of Genesis mean to say"). The appeal seems, in fact, to be part of Barth's use of parallel passages (to be discussed below). The 'intentionality' brought to bear on an ambiguous passage is the expositor's judgement--usually in the light of traditional ecclesial exegesis--concerning what the remaining texts (of an "author", book, or the Bible as a whole) press one to expect from a disputed reading. Whatever the case may be in fact, the appeal is always offered as compelling and precise. And finally, because the appeal is not "historical" in the usual sense, Barth uses traditional names and the traditional scope for the corpus of an author; i.e., "Paul" means the canonical Pauline corpus--even including the speeches of Paul in Acts (e.g., II.1, pp. 118-123).

Having discussed some aspects of the Bible as a text in Barth's exegesis, we turn now more particularly to this text as a witness, though delaying for the moment consideration of that to which it bears witness. The Bible is a witness; most comprehensively this means that the Bible always has something to say, and that what it says it says in attestation of revelation. Consider, for example, the following excursus from II.1 (pp. 411-16); the doctrinal point under discussion is the view that God's patience with respect to human sin and wretchedness implies no limitation or weakness, but is in fact the very essence of God's almighty power. As Barth introduces the exegesis: "We shall see at once that this patience is the divine being in power and not in weakness if we consider in detail the testimony (*Zeugnis*) of Scripture to God's revelation from this particular standpoint." Notice that from the outset Barth's exegesis presupposes that the Bible has something to say about such a doctrinal detail of the Christian confession. He then proceeds with an exposition of the story of Cain (Gen. 4.1-17), the story of Noah (Gen. 6-9), and the book of Jonah. In each case he asserts that the biblical passage has a point or theme, and that the point or theme is essentially identical with the doctrinal concept under discussion. My concern is not to argue that Barth is thus reading the Bible as a doctrinal textbook, or reading into it Christian confessional concerns. He quite clearly claims to find in the text the exact, detailed point he is trying to make. My point is rather that Barth does indeed look for a theme or point, and one which functions as a witness to divine revelation. Other ways of reading the text, and other aspects of the text such as its literary form, its historical origin, its social background and foreground, even its "theology" *per se* are subordinated to the one focal point of its place in the comprehensive biblical witness to the Word of God. Again, this is not to suggest that Barth looks right past the literary forms of the Bible. I shall argue in a later chapter that he does not; and precisely in the exegetical passage under discussion he reads narrative material from Genesis as narrative and the book of Jonah as prophecy. What I here argue is that all such considerations, and indeed all detailed exegetical considerations generally, are strictly subordinate to the focal exegetical concern of finding in the text a witness. This *function* of the text governs all other exegetical considerations, questions, procedures.

To read the Bible as a witness to the Word of God is to construe it, as a whole and in each of its books and individual passages, as a divinely commissioned human response to a prior *act* of divine revelation. Two examples will help make this statement more clear, and will illustrate the direct bearing it has on the actual exegesis of a biblical text. The first example, from I.1, is an exegetical excursus on New Testament passages concerning Jesus Christ's divine-humanity, and occurs in a section of the *Church Dogmatics* on Christology and the Trinity (pp. 402-6). The question Barth raises, after simply quoting the New Testament statements concerning Christ's divinity, is simply this: how does one construe these statements exegetically in such a way that one's construal corresponds to the standpoint of the New Testament itself?   One dominant approach in modern Protestantism has been to ask of these texts how it came about that knowledge of the historical figure of Jesus was transformed into faith in a heavenly Son of God.   The New Testament texts are then construed as apostolic *interpretation* of the figure of Jesus, the cause of the transformation being explained as either the impact of Jesus' personality (so great that he can only be divine), or the compelling hold of a collective idea as applied to an impressive individual (in this man we find embodied our idea of God).   Either way--through apotheosis of a man or through the application of a collective myth, through personality or idea--the transformation is construed as interpretation, and individual New Testament texts are read as evidence for the history of culture.   As opposed to this construal, Barth offers the concept of *witness*: "The New Testament statement about Christ's deity makes sense only as witness to God's revelation. Any other exegesis is blatantly opposed to the opinion of the authors and in conflict with them" (p. 404). Granted that there are in the New Testament basically ascending elements ("this man became God"), and basically descending elements ("God became this man"), these two directions of New Testament thought are misunderstood unless they are construed as deriving from a third direction which is the logical starting point for both: the directly present reality of the God-man Jesus Christ, teaching and healing, dying and rising again among them. This *fact* of divine revelation is the actual and logical starting point for New Testament confession; the New Testament statements concerning the God-man Jesus Christ are rightly construed only as witnesses to the Word of God, as the uninterpreted assertion of a directly present, and hence self-clarifying, divine-human fact. There was no transformation because there was no interpretation, and there was no interpretation because the two elements of New Testament confession had no need of being brought together in either of two movements of thought: they had no need because they were never in fact apart. To read the New Testament this way is to read it as witness.

The second example comes from an exegetical excursus in II.1 on the doctrine of the divine perfections (pp. 451-457). Passages from both Testaments are adduced, in correspondence with the doctrinal theme under discussion, attesting the uniqueness of God. Again, the exegetical question Barth raises is how to construe such passages. He discusses the possibility of a familiar option--that of monotheistic theism--which reads these passages in the light of "natural theology." In such an approach, the biblical statements are construed as the intellectual juxtaposition and synthesis of two ideas--the idea of the divine and the idea of uniqueness--in human thought. Against this reading Barth offers the way of witness, which juxtaposes these two concepts *actually* (*"faktisch"*) and not merely *verbally* (*"verbal"*) (*K.D.*, p. 511). In other words, the confession that God is unique in the Bible is construed as the uninterpreted attestation of a divine self-demonstration and self-explanation. The theological exegesis of biblical texts does not ask of these words what experience they express--though they can of course be addressed with this question--but rather what truth of God's revelation they attest. Asked the one question they yield one answer; asked the other, they yield a witness to God's Word.

The whole Bible--constituted as such by the one self-attesting Spirit--is a witness to the Word of God. But, does every passage, every verse, carry this one message? Does a fact of revelation present itself at every turn in the Bible? How many facts of revelation are there: one? several? one in several? Why a "fact" or "event" of revelation at all? Isn't such a conception uniquely appropriate to narrative discourse? These and other questions are raised by my analysis of Barth's exegesis under the concept "witness," and will be addressed in due course. For the present, however, I should like to identify a conceptual-exegetical move sometimes made in Barth's exegesis which renders the concept witness more elastic than it otherwise might be. Firstly, not every strand of biblical literature is straightforwardly witness. It is necessary to realize, however, that when this is the case--when, that is, a passage of the Bible appears unrelated to the central biblical function--it is exegetically to be brought into relation to this function. Or rather, it is exegetically to be recognized that it has already assumed this function by its presence in the Bible despite its immanent characteristics. For example, when arguing against the concept of the analogy of being in natural theology in II.1, Barth concedes the presence in the Bible of several passages (e.g. the "Nature Psalms") suspiciously like natural theology, and devoid, therefore, of any witness to a fact of divine revelation (pp. 97-176). They are numerous enough to constitute a "side line" to the "main line" of the biblical witness. Barth's solution? Quite simply to insist that, when expounding such passages, they must always be systematically subordinated in intent and meaning to the main line of biblical witness. They are witness, because they must be brought into relation to witness. Or rather, it must be seen that they have been brought into such a relation; Barth never once, to my knowledge, offers an exegesis of a biblical passage that suggests it must by *made* to bear witness. He rather at times suggests that great care must be taken to recognize the place of a passage in the Bible as a whole, lest the concealed relation of a passage to the biblical witness remain unnoticed. There is witness in the Bible, and there is for the moment concealed witness; there is not something else altogether--at least from the point of view of theological exegesis. The revelation to which the Bible bears witness has a form, has an inner order, as discerned from the inner order of the biblical witness itself. We noticed above the problem of the presence of seemingly alien material in this witness; we now raise the question of the *absence* of material in support of central moments in the overall form of God's Word. What happens when a central concept of Barth's doctrine of divine revelation is relatively absent from the biblical testimony-- whence alone any doctrine ought to come? Just as there is *concealed* witness, so there is *implied* witness; witness to God's Word can be present in a passage by implication, as if the reader is called to fill in the spaces of a familiar picture when one finds an incomplete rendition. For example, the concept of election (II.2, pp. 146-55) is a comprehensive concept throughout the Bible, though passages directly attesting it are actually quite few. God's sovereign grace in election is a central aspect of Barth's concept of the Word of God; though it is discussed rarely in the Bible, it is attested in such a way as to make clear its central importance for the biblical message. Therefore, account must be taken of it in the exegesis of all passages of the Bible--whether it is directly present or not. For example, individual characters who come and go throughout the pages of the Bible are assumed to come under the scope of this concept, whether mention is made or not of their divine election or rejection (p. 341). This is implied witness, and together with concealed witness as treated above, it allows Barth the kind of focus with flexibility that his exegetical and doctrinal approach requires.

Example A: The Divine Choice

We turn now to the first in our series of examples for close analysis. In order to correspond with the wide-ranging subject of this first chapter, it was necessary to choose an example with a wide variety of exegetical concerns; for this purpose I have selected for analysis the excursus supporting Barth's doctrine of the election of the individual (*C.D.* II.2, pp. 354-409).[2] While unified in scope and conceptual interest, the excursus actually contains four separate pieces of exegesis, each of which will receive attention below. They are: certain paired figures in the patriarchal narratives, passages from Leviticus 14 and 16, the traditions concerning Saul and David, and I Kings 13. Except that they are all from the Old Testament, the passages seem to share little else formally and historically; they are nevertheless read as a united witness by Barth. At this stage of the analysis of these exegetical passages--the analysis will continue later in the chapter--our attention will be focused on Barth's exegesis of these passages as *texts* bearing *witness*. We shall later return to inquire *how* they bear witness, and *what* it is they attest.

The theme for the entire excursus is sounded immediately in the exegesis of certain figures in Genesis, beginning with Cain and Abel. Three aspects of this story interest Barth. Firstly, God's prevenient choice governs the acceptability or not of their respective offerings. Secondly, God's marking of Cain implies a kind of relative election within a relative rejection; there is here no absolute rejection. And finally, because Abel, though elected, finds only death, and Cain, though rejected, finds a guaranteed life, the absolute distinction between the characters is blurred;

---

[2]Ford comments on this excursus in *Barth and God's Story*, pp. 79-84.

Abel and Cain become conceptually necessary to one another. One cannot tell the story of an elected Abel without telling of the rejected Cain, nor can one hold up the rejected Cain without including the elected Abel. Barth calls this passage the classical example of the principles of election just mentioned. That is, he claims that the curious crisscrossing relations of election and rejection found in this passage should govern one's reading of biblical situations of individual election and rejection. To illustrate, he traces briefly a line of similarly matched pairs of characters throughout Genesis, including Isaac and Ishmael, Esau and Jacob, Rachel and Leah, and Ephraim and Manasseh. Through it all, God's choice precedes and makes relative all human choices, situations, and predilections. And for all the sharply drawn distinction between elect and rejected, some sign of blessing always finds the rejected, while the elect are hardly obviously so in the customary sense. The stories need both characters to make their points; without either character, the stories would be very different, and would point off in a different direction.

Notice here the seemingly obvious; the biblical passages make a *point* that Barth's exegesis is able conceptually to isolate and highlight--and without violence to the texts, or so the exegesis implies. But the "point" is not something different from the texts, not a second thing which one has to talk about once one has offered a more straightforward exegesis. This is why so much of Barth's exegesis is quite literally re-telling; in this instance, as in many others, complete with strings of quotation. Barth finds a theme in a passage, and it is not surprising that the theme corresponds to a doctrinal point under discussion. Nevertheless, the theme does not hover above the passage, nor can it be abstracted from it; the passage itself constitutes the theme. But obviously (or is it always obvious in Barth's exegesis?) it is the passage read a certain way. This way is witness. What does the story of Cain and Abel, and the paired figures in Genesis generally, have to say about God's Word, God's revelation? What witness does it bear? In the first instance, the answer is the simple content of the texts themselves read as witness; they speak of God's sovereign election and rejection within election of these mutually necessary individuals.

We turn next to Barth's exegesis of two passages from Old Testament law, Lev. 14.4-7 and Lev. 16.5ff. The first concerns a ceremony related to the cleansing of a leper, the second an aspect of the ritual day of atonement. It is noteworthy that Barth chooses to exegete these together at all; it seems clear that whatever they share must be hidden from the reader except by the intervention of an expositor. And yet Barth claims to find a common, even complementary, witness in the passages by reading them not in the light of their narrower contexts (cleansing of leper, day of atonement--neither of which is mentioned again), nor in view of their broader contexts (ritual law, or even Law), but in the light of the narratives of Genesis! These two passages are in fact a commentary on the binary election/rejection stories of Genesis, and must be so read if they are to provide their witness to the Word of God.

The passages share a common structure, and it is this local structure (not part of the broader literary context) which serves up the meaning. In Lev. 14, a bird is ritually killed and another released, and indeed the first for the sake of the second. In Lev. 16, a goat is killed and another released, the first for its own sake, the latter released only to death in life. The common structure is the binary opposition of choice; one animal is chosen, another is rejected, in neither case depending on innate usability. The stories differ, however, in that in Lev. 14

the rejected animal is freed for life by the death of the elected, while in Lev. 16 the elect animal must die and the rejected is set free--though only to a non-life. Notice, then, the full pattern. A choice is made beyond all innate qualifications; nevertheless, the destiny of the elect and the rejected is relativized. Barth finds in this structure a witness concerning the full meaning of the narratives of Genesis. When we read these passages as witness, we are to think of Cain and Abel, Jacob and Esau, etc., and to see in the figures of the animals the characters in the stories.

The exegetical procedure used by Barth here is not really allegory (there are no abstract moral qualities or abstract doctrinal motifs) nor typology proper (which interrelates two or more narratives) nor the *sensus literalis* of the Reformation (--though Barth quotes Calvin, and alludes to "the older Christian exegesis," a mere glance at Calvin's commentary will show that the two have nothing whatsoever in common). It is perhaps akin to structuralism in its interest in a hidden structure of a binary nature, though the foundational context for interpretation is not a social or anthropological theory but another narrative, indeed another biblical narrative! That it is another *narrative* is perhaps important, though not, I think, the key: Barth interprets Genesis *narrative*, as we shall see, in the light of New Testament *doctrine* (Pauline, not the gospels'). Not allegory, nor typology, nor *sensus literalis*; not structuralism, nor narrative theology.

That Barth reroutes the passages through the narratives of Genesis is unusual with respect to Christian exegetical tradition; that he reaches the final destination of a pure Christological reference is not. His method of doing this as well is in direct contrast to, say, an approach like Calvin's, and we shall return to this method later in the chapter. Here we shall point out the exegetical point of departure for the final stage of his exegesis. Both passages have been placed in the interpretive context of Genesis narratives; the animals are therefore figures for elect and rejected people. The pairs are, however, so closely related conceptually that they press toward a single reference to a single person. But what single person? Certainly not a figure in Genesis; nowhere in Genesis does a single figure even begin to comprehend the crisscrossing relations of election and rejection, life and death necessitated by our passages. Where then? To what unitary subject do these passages point? And what Old Testament life, what Old Testament death, can bear the significance of the life and death of these animals as figures of elect and rejected people? Both these questions--the question of unity, and the anomaly of the subject matter--are like signals encoded in the text, signals that tell the reader that the witness of the text points to a beyond remote from the text. We halt here at the signals themselves; we shall later return to the object of their witness, and how it is arrived at.

We consider, thirdly, Barth's exposition of the figures of Saul and David in the Old Testament (*C.D.* pp. 366-393). Barth is clearly not interested in abstracting a "character" from the flow of Old Testament narrative for isolated consideration. He intends, rather, to consider these two figures in the full concretion of their narrated world and individual place; he only focuses this intention by highlighting a certain perspective on the figures within the text. Or rather, he follows the Old Testament as it does the highlighting by the presence of I Sam. 8 at the head of all the material on the two kings, and the kingship generally. Barth finds in this leading chapter two principal points: that the people desire a king only in wickedness and folly; that God desires a king for his gracious purpose. The absolute conflict of these desires, and the mystery surrounding the final goal of the divine purpose, push along all that follows.

Once again, Barth finds in the stories of Saul and David a pattern corresponding to the comprehensive theme of this section of the *Dogmatics*. God's election is absolutely supreme, beyond all human predisposition; yet while supreme, it is not absolute, unyielding, impervious; the living reality of God controls the relation--the relation does not control the living reality of God. The figure of Saul is above all a figure of darkness; Saul is rejected by God as the righteous king on the basis of a series of sins which cannot in themselves justify such rejection. The rejection proceeds forth from God's hand, not from Saul's "microscopic" faults. And yet while rejected, there is a "Davidic" side to Saul--he too is the true king of Israel, willed by God in his own way, and as such a figure of relative light and honor and glory.

David, on the other hand, is primarily a figure of light--the elect king, God's true king. And he remains this despite the most heinous of sins--heinous in God's eyes as well as our own, because they amount to a rejection of God's ideal kingship in favor of the typical pattern and habits of the pagan king. Yet through it all David's election stands firm, because it is *God's* election. Nevertheless, there is a Saul-side to David-- after his sin, his monarchy becomes a typical human monarchy, filled with the darkness of palace intrigue (Absalom) and deferred promise.

Barth is aware that the material he is dealing with may come from differing sources, and may also go back to two or more circles of tradition. He mentions these possibilities (p. 372) only to sharpen the perception that the two characters are only meaningful together. Saul is absolutely necessary to the unfolding plot; God chooses a Saul in order to purge and punish the incipient rebellion at Ramah (I. Sam. 8). Without Saul there would be no David; just as, without David the figure of Saul would point nowhere, would lead forward into no future. The figures of Saul and David are conceptually necessary to one another. And so we have here the same criss-crossing, relativized relations of election and rejection as in the other passages we have considered. We have as well signals in the text that the exegesis cannot stop here, that that to which the text bears witness is not found directly in the witness as we have so far presented it. To this aspect of Barth's exegesis we shall return later.

We turn, finally, to Barth's exegesis of I Kings 13 concerning the man of God from Judah and the old prophet of Bethel in the days of Jeroboam (pp. 393-409). The historical-critical problems receive some small attention--Barth considers the passage to be "drawn from another source than its context" (p. 393)--though they are raised as an aid in answering the question of the "real subject" of this chapter. Notice the obvious, though highly significant: the chapter has a "real subject" which exegesis must lay bare and explore. In order to accomplish this task Barth proceeds through four stages of analysis. He firstly divides the material literarily into a series of five sections and a provisional epilogue, the final epilogue being delayed until II Kings 23. 15-20. No supporting evidence is offered for his actual divisions; they are certainly not in the nature of source divisions or the like, nor are they justified in light of different literary options (e.g., neither the Zuerich Bible nor Luther's Bible have Barth's divisions). Barth seems to offer them as natural and obvious units of the overall plot.

Barth then divides the story further into a series of three crises: the prophet's lie to the man of God, the prophet's proclamation of the Word of the Lord, and the prophet's care for the dead man of God. The crises entail a series of role-reversals: the prophet first takes the place of the man of God as authentic spokesman for God, while the man of God sins; then the prophet acknowledges the enduring superiority of the calling of the man of God--he hastens to bury him in order to create for himself a refuge in God's blessing of the man of God. Five literary sections containing three crises; notice the patience Barth has with the text as a text.

And yet he proceeds beyond such a controlled, measured re-telling. The series of crisscrossing relations brought forth in the three main crises yield a structure, or a picture--in this case a dual picture. On the right is the picture of the man of God from Judah, blessed with the Word of God and the promise of grace, and yet finally rebellious and cast violently into the grave. On the left is the old prophet of Bethel, a sham prophet of a rejected nation, and yet blessed with the Word of God and the hope of a future in the grave of the man of God. Barth seizes on this dual picture as such for the message, the "real subject," the *witness* of the chapter. What it wants to say it says by painting this picture of the elected and the rejected, the man of God and the old prophet.

And finally, Barth completes the analysis by pointing out the complementary relationship of the two figures in the story. Each is a kind of mirror image of the other, yet the firm rule of divine election and rejection is never broken. God rejects, God elects; and yet the result of this divine rule is not dualistic, but dialectical; not fatalistic, but flexible; not the steady, unchanging, absolute condition of death, but the fluid and relative uncertainty of life. This is the witness of the text. But the text is this witness; it does not contain it like a vessel contains a substance. It is a question of reading the text the right way, not reading the text and then doing something else. But has Barth read the text the right way? To this question he offers no answer; he

barely acknowledges the question itself.   This much is
certain, and it follows from his approach as detailed
above: the question cannot be asked, from Barth's point
of view, as formal inquiry, but can be posited only by
offering a different reading, a different exegesis.   This
possibility Barth acknowledges, but only just; the
question of the commensurability of two readings, and
the proper way to choose one or the other, is left
unasked.

As with the previous pieces of exegesis in this
excursus, Barth does not stop here with his analysis of I
Kings 13.   He has analyzed the text, and located the
witness in the text; he has yet to move from the witness
to its object.   In this case, as in the others, we shall
postpone consideration of this movement until later in
the chapter.

The Witness as Word

The subject matter of Holy Scripture is witness to
God's Word.   As such it has two dimensions: a textual
content and a real *object*.   The former we have
previously discussed; to the latter we now turn for the
remainder of this chapter.   We begin with what the
object of the biblical witness is *not*.   It is neither an
ideal nor historical referent.   That is, there is no access
to the object of this text apart from the text itself.   A
disjunction of the text and its object for whatever
purpose--perhaps for the purpose, say, of placing the
object of the text in a conceptual matrix different from
that offered by the text itself--is not what Barth is
after when in his exegesis he searches for the object of
the biblical witness.   The object of the text is *real*--
Barth often calls the search for it the "truth-question" in
exegesis and theology--though the entire conceptual
apparatus   of   ostensive   reference,   in   any   of   its

theological forms (conservative or liberal), is useless for what Barth does with a text.[3] So, what is the 'object' of a biblical text? If it is one thing--and Barth often speaks as though it is--it is the event of God's reconciling and revealing Word in Jesus Christ. It is the mysterious divine act of God's presence to humankind in the person of Jesus Christ. Now, much of Barth's exegesis ends up tending toward, if not directly dealing with, these central concepts of what Barth calls the Word of God revealed. Much of it, however, does not, or does so only indirectly. And it is difficult to decide whether Barth often misrepresents his own position, or whether certain concepts and words are to be taken rather loosely (i.e., the *one* Word of God in Jesus Christ ends up being 9,000 pages worth of "one"), or again whether Barth was unsure of his position and actually held two or more views. There is *enormous* variety in Barth's biblical exegesis: more so than one is lead to expect by his programmatic statements. We shall examine the Christological aspect of this problem in the next chapter; for now I simply wish to assert that the variety is encompassed by a comprehensive unity. The texts of the Bible are about many things for Barth; they are nevertheless all related to one comprehensive "thing"--God's revelation in Jesus Christ. The variety is thus not in ultimate conflict, presumably, with the unity. However, there are two very different ways in which Barth arrives at this unity--a problem to which we shall return below.

Again, there is an object, or objects, or objects in an Object, after which exegesis strives in its approach to the biblical text. We have previously examined the textual element; how, that is, one analyzes a text to find in it and listen to its witness. We are now commenting

---

[3] The background to this paragraph can be found in the now standard Hans. W. Frei, *The Eclipse of Biblical Narrative* (New Haven and London: Yale University Press, 1974).

on what one hears, on the object that presents itself. What is the relation of the text to its object, the witness to that to which it bears witness? A good comprehensive concept would be *depiction*: the text *depicts* its object. Barth uses many ideas: the text refers, it points, it attests; the text pictures, it mirrors, and so forth; all of them seem related to the general notion of depiction. Or, one can use Barth's own general statement: "Purely formally, the revelation to which the biblical witnesses direct their gaze as they look and point away from themselves is to be distinguished from the word of the witnesses in exactly the same way as an event itself is to be distinguished from even the best and most faithful account of it" (*C.D.* I.1, p. 113). The text depicts this event.

Barth calls the distinction between the text as account and the Word as event "purely formal" for a very important reason: the object of this text has a voice. It is alive; it speaks. And herein lies *the* logical conundrum in Barth's exegesis of the Bible. We are to search for this object, even as it seeks us. However, we have this object available to us *solely* through Holy Scripture; no outside appeal of whatever sort--even an appeal to our experience of this object as we hear it in Scripture--can be called to judge when and where we have correctly found this object in Scripture. We must read the text to find *this object*; but we have only *the text* to tell us what this object is. The logical circle is as obvious as it is, from Barth's point of view, impervious. Or rather, it is broken only by the object itself; but again, that is equivalent to saying "by exegesis." The problem of exegesis is solved by exegesis, which in turn must always be a "problem" in light of its object.

What is the "problem" of exegesis? It is clearly created by the distinction between the text and its object; why make this distinction at all? For Barth, the distinction is already there before us, and is made by the object itself. The object of the text is divine; the text itself is human, even while it is divinely authorized. The distinction--and with it the "problem" set for exegesis--is already there before us in that the living God is far greater than any human attempt to bear witness to Him. But notice that the emphasis is on *God's* greatness, not on human poverty, though the latter is surely entailed. The text of the Bible, the language of its witness, is not distant from its divine Object because human language, and with it biblical language, is *fallen*. The problematic of exegesis is not created by the poverty of language. There is here no *Sprachskepsis*, theological or otherwise. The text of the Bible is, rather, distant from its Divine Object because of this Object. The problematic of exegesis is created by the glory of the living God. And the resulting *Skepsis* is directed neither toward the Object, nor toward the text as such, but toward the *reader*. The technical language Barth uses to discuss this problem is the language of *analogy* (II.1 pp. 216-54).

The biblical writers used the common languages at their disposal in bearing witness to God's Word. Though God's great glory immediately creates a distance from their witness, His gracious presence to them overcomes this barrier, nor does it do so violently; for as the Creator of human language, in coming to human language, God in some sense comes to His own. But for us who are dependent on their witness the distance remains, and must be overcome again and again in the exegesis of the Bible. The problem this creates is at the same time both a technical problem of biblical exegesis and the profound but ultimately unanalyzable question whether God will indeed again be present to us who seek Him in His Word. There is no way to ask the latter question apart from exegesis, nor does its answer precede, accompany, or follow the exegetical hearing of the Word of God in the Bible; it is, rather, this hearing in its true sense.

But the technical question of *analogy* in exegesis remains. Notice again that it is directed toward the *reader* rather than toward the *text*, or its *object*. The doctrine of analogy states the conceptual, semantic (in other schools, though not in Barth, the metaphysical, ontological) relation between statements about God and statements about the world and persons in it using the same linguistic utterances ("God is good," "John is good"). The Bible uses common language in its witness to God's revelation. Now, the burden of Barth's doctrine of analogy, and the actual thrust of his exegesis, is to argue that the method and goal of exegesis is *not* to manipulate, to translate, to handle--to *ply* the *text* of the Bible to get to its object. The point is rather to ply the *reader*--oneself--till the Bible can again serve up its message. Or rather, it is God who plies the reader thus. The words of the Bible say what they mean and mean what they say; it is the *reader* who uses these common words in a way that needs purging in the light of the biblical texts. The primary analogate is the text of the Bible as witness; the secondary, problematic analogate is the text of the Bible in the ears of a reader problematically related to the object of its witness (as every reader is). The flow of interpretation is thus from the Bible to the reader, not from the reader to the Bible.

Such a view of analogy in biblical language has enormous consequences for all of Barth's exegesis. It is the basis for his rejection of any kind of systematically pursued "pre-understanding" in reading the Bible. And more importantly for our purposes, it accounts for the enormous amount of time and space Barth uses to show the reader, and himself, around in the text of the Bible. "What the Bible says" is not the starting point for further exegetical and theological reflection ahead of the text;

it is rather the *goal* of all exegesis. Enormous energy is not to be used doing something with "what the Bible says"; enormous energy and endless patience are required in simply finding it out! The finding of it is at the end of the process of exegesis, as well as at its beginning. Indeed it is the end, though this end is in some ways never finally reached once for all. An example of this process is Barth's exegesis of various biblical passages in support of his doctrine of divine predicates. Here, as many times elsewhere in the *Church Dogmatics*, Barth rejects the notion of "anthropomorphism" as an exegetical tool--and not just in its many modern forms, such as historical critical history of religions, but also in its classical Christian forms--patristic, medieval, protestant scholastic. Over and over again one reads "this is not metaphor," or "this is to be taken literally, not figuratively" or the like in Barth's exegesis of passages widely considered "anthropomophisms" (cf. II.1, p. 263, 475, 479, 498 among others). In each case the point is this: a given passage of the Bible is widely assumed to be problematically related to its object by virtue of the anthropomorphic dimensions of its depiction. The object of exegesis is thus to translate--in any of a number of ways, ancient and modern--what the Bible says in order to arrive at a proper knowledge of its divine object. Barth's exegesis says *no*; the goal is simply to find what the Bible says-- it needs no translation. What needs changing is the *reader's* conception of some supposedly "anthropomorphic" divine ascription. When the Bible speaks of God changing his mind, I am to realize that the problem of exegesis is created by lack of knowledge of a living God who changes His mind freely, not by my knowledge that God can't really "change His mind." There *is* and *always* is a problem; otherwise I easily, and wrongly, assume that when God changes His mind it is the same as when I do, or an acquaintance does. The biblical witness that God changes His mind is problematic, but the statement itself remains constant throughout exegesis, and knowledge of its content is the goal--what needs changing is the reader's knowledge of God (pp. 485-499).

Barth deploys a variety of methods to locate the object of the witness of a text or texts. None of the ways seems predominate. He firstly locates the object by the conceptual analysis of a single lexical item over large ranges of biblical material. He starts with as much variety as he can find, and slowly works toward a unified concept--the object of these texts. For example, he analyzes the New Testament uses of "faith" by carefully charting the varied nuances based on usage in John, Paul, the Synoptics, . . . etc. He proceeds, however, toward a single reality--faith as the knowledge of God. The single reality is larger than any single text; it is nevertheless present in every text, and seemingly without depressing the nuances provides the condition for the possibility of these being nuances of a single reality at all: "In reality, however, all these meanings of the term stand under a common denominator" (I.1, pp. 228-9). Barth can similarly move from several texts to one reality by analysis not of a single lexical item, but a more broadly defined concept. The method is here the same as the study of a word, only the selection of texts for analysis depends on the presence of a general concept. For example Barth provides an analysis of "the name of God" in both Old and New Testament texts at a crucial juncture of his presentation of the doctrine of revelation (I.1, pp. 316-19). There is of course less control over the choice of texts for analysis, and the resulting unpredictability gives these excursuses a slightly different aspect than the methodologically identical word studies.

Barth can also proceed by the conceptual analysis of a single passage, moving toward a single reality. I call the analysis 'conceptual' because, among other reasons, such pieces of exegesis usually search for a single point, or concept, as a clue in the witness of the passage as to its true object. Barth almost never gives an exegesis in which he finds several concepts or theological points, though the major concept or concepts are always found amidst an enormous variety of exegetical detail. Even with several pages of exegesis on a single text the yield is one or a few conceptual points--usually just one. For example, Barth expounds the pericope of the Good Samaritan, and finds in this one text the reality of "the neighbor" (II.1, pp. 417-19).

Barth will also find the object of the biblical witness in the juxtaposition of two or more passages, whether individual passages or larger blocks of material. He never finds the object in a complete antithesis of two or more texts, nor in a complete synthesis. He will at times stress the antithetical elements, as when he stresses the one-sidedness of the concept of the covenant in Ex. 19-20 and Jer. 31 (I.1, pp. 179-81). Or, he can stress the more complementary aspects, as in his presentation of New Testament Christology (I.2, pp. 13-25). But it is never more than a question of emphasis; one text is never set at war with another, nor are texts ever synthetically reduced beyond recognition. The key is always to move from the varied texts, whether more antithetical or more complementary, to a single reality, without drawing attention away from the particularities of the texts as such, even if the particularities point in different, or directly opposing, directions. Such a view of course *assumes* a single object to such texts, an assumption which flies in the face of certain other approaches (such as the historical-critical method, or Marcion's approach, etc.)

Finally, Barth can find the object of the biblical witness not so much in a single text, or even a variety of texts, as in the background, the assumption, the condition for these texts. This method is used least of all, but it can of course occur at crucial points. Its inherent lack of control--no one text or texts contain the point Barth is trying to make exegetically, so surely the object is at best harder to see--together with the pivotal role it can play, make excursuses of this sort the most obvious targets for the familiar charge of "proof-texting." For example, various aspects of Barth's doctrine of predestination, and particularly its Christological form, are often supported exegetically by pronouncement of "implied concepts" or "rules" which more nearly govern biblical usage than occur in it (e.g., II.2, p. 191). In such instances it is as if the witness and the object are the same thing, which supports the view that Barth is here really starting with the object and finding a witness--or at least the broad traces of one.

The terminus of Barth's exegesis is always the object attested by the witness of the text. The relation of the text to this terminus can, however, be direct, or it can be more indirect. In his exegesis of Psalm 40 Barth states--concedes really--that the text is spoken by a member of the later Jewish church. But later verses in the Psalm about confession and forgiveness are a clue, Barth argues, that the text has as well a hidden meaning, a meaning in which the speaker of the Psalm points away from himself. In light of well-known verses from Jer. 31, Ezek. 11 and 36, and Rom. 2, Barth further argues that the hidden reference is in fact eschatological; the Psalm points forward to a hidden subject. And yet it must be stressed: the verses "are to be understood eschatologically in essence, although without prejudice to their concrete content" (II.2, p. 604). The terminal object is arrived at through correct attention to an intermediary object. The intermediary object--in this case the believing prayer of the faithful Jew--does not, however, completely lose all reality, as if moving from shadow to substance.   If the intermediary recedes, it is more like a ladder which is cast aside once its function has been performed; once, that is, one has arrived (cf. II.2, pp 604-6 for the exegesis).   We here only raise the problem of a direct or indirect terminus; the form it takes is uniformly Christological, and we shall therefore postpone fuller discussion until the next chapter.

Barth continues his exegesis of Ps. 40 by hinting that it presses toward its true subject--Jesus Christ (pp. 605-6).   Jesus Christ in some sense becomes the true Speaker of this Psalm.   He alone can truly say that of Him it is written in the roll of God's book.   Such a move is highly characteristic of Barth: the terminus of his exegesis tends toward Jesus Christ.   One is forced to ask, then, whether the Bible is really about only one thing; whether, that is, all its seeming variety is a veil behind which stands one Object alone.   Are there objects in Barth's exegesis, or an Object?   Given the above distinction between a direct and an indirect terminus it becomes possible to say a great deal while ultimately saying only one thing.   Is this how Barth's exegesis sounds?   The answer to these questions again depends on one's estimation of the Christological focus of Barth's exegesis, to which we shall shortly turn.

We have now concluded our summary analysis of the main contours of Barth's biblical exegesis under the concept "witness."   We have discussed aspects of his exegesis of the text as witness, his exegetical search for the object of the text, and the relation between the witness and its true object.   There remains only to ask: why "witness" at all?   Why does Barth read the Bible this way?   Rather strangely, at first glance, Barth offers very little in the way of an answer to this question.   He offers only the "obvious" fact that in the Bible there is an "unusual preponderance of what is said . . . over the word as such" (I.2, p. 468). Now, this sentence--and it really is just a sentence, not a small piece of extended argument--could mean any of several things, some of which correspond to Barth's actual exegesis, while others do not. I consider it useless to speculate in this instance; the point Barth is perhaps trying to make is too unclear, too ambiguous, to be of any help. And yet he offers such a gnomic argument as if it were obvious to all. This latter fact is more important than the argument (or absence of one) itself: Barth offers his exegesis of the Bible as a witness to the Word of God as if everybody could see that this is just what the Bible itself obviously requires. He does not so much offer it as obviously *right*; he rather offers it as obviously *biblical*, as, that is, an exegesis which, if wrong, is nonetheless on the right track even if it sometimes misses the point.

I said above that the lack of argument for "witness" in Barth is 'at first glance' surprising. By that I meant that there is, upon reflection, something right about the absence of supporting argument for Barth's exegesis of the Bible. As discussed earlier in the chapter, the exegesis, including the comprehensive approach to the Bible which it entails, is "self-confirming" (or indeed "self-denying") in light of the mutual fit of text, object, and reader. Discussion of the appropriateness or not of a piece of exegesis can only take place by further exegesis--hence Barth's oft-repeated challenge to negate his exegesis by offering a better one (see e.g. II.2, p. 393). The world of Barth's exegesis of the Bible is so large that it includes *within* it the reasons for *entering* it. Or, it is so small that it drives away all but the partisan few. In suggesting these two different ways of seeing the logic of Barth's approach we here come up against a wall separating two comprehensive visions of argument generally; it cannot be the purpose of this dissertation to breach this wall.

Example A (continued)

We return now to the analysis of our first example from Barth's exegesis: the excursus containing an exegesis of the patriarchal narratives, Lev. 14 and 16, David and Saul, and I Kings 13, within the context of the doctrine of election.   The exegesis of the patriarchal narratives, in which Barth finds the witness by locating a crisscrossing pattern of binary opposition based on God's prevenient decision, moves *directly* from the witness to the object.   The object of the text is the characters so related to God and to each other.   The "principle" of distinguishing choice governs the tradition's rendering, but it is not the "principle" itself which constitutes the object of this witness.   Neither is is the characters as such, nor presumed or reconstructed historical figures behind the characters; that is, the text is not about the characters *per se*, the principle of election being an "interpretation" or the like.   It is rather about the characters in the meaningful relation they sustain to one another and in which they are sustained by and to God.

We return now to the exegesis of the rituals involved in the cure of a leper and the day of atonement in Lev. 14 and 16 (pp. 357-366).   Recall that Barth locates the witness of these passages by relating the ritual animals in the text (the birds and the goats) to the individual human characters in other parts of the Bible, especially the patriarchal narratives.   These characters, related to each other and to God after the pattern of election and rejection typified in the ritual actions, are indeed the object of the witness.   The text is about these characters, or individuals like them, and tends to say of them what other parts of the Bible say of them.   Barth will carry his exegesis of these passages further; had he, however, simply stopped at this point in his treatment-- and even, in some sense, though he continues--one must surely ask why the Lev. passages are there at all, or are worthy of exegetical attention, if their content is really only the content of another passage or passages. Such a question can be directed at many streams of the tradition of typological (and allegorical) exegesis, and will be pressed further in a later chapter.

But Barth does not halt his exegesis of Lev. 14 and 16 by moving toward its object in individual election; these texts, in fact, surprise the reader by imbuing the animals--and hence the typologically intended individual elect and rejected--with fantastic powers of redemptive life and death. If one grants that the ritual animals and actions of Lev. 14 and 16 point toward individual elect and rejected persons as their object, then one is forced to conclude that, while the passages do cohere in large measure with the Old Testament matrix to which they are related, they also go far beyond it. Nowhere in the Old Testament are individual persons so elected, nowhere so rejected; nowhere is an individual death so full of redemption, and yet equally accursed; nowhere an individual life so full of grace. The individual life and death typified by these animals is ultimately inscrutable to the Old Testament universe of discourse. Therefore, the object of these texts cannot ultimately be individual elect and rejected people as they occur in the Old Testament, as in the patriarchal narratives. Such Old Testament individuals are the mediate object of the text, but they are not the terminal object. Indeed, the Old Testament universe of discourse can only tell us *that* there is a terminal object; the Old Testament itself cannot yield the object which the Old Testament says these texts must have. And, of course, the terminus of these texts is in fact the person of Jesus Christ, and they say about Him more or less what familiar

New Testament--especially Pauline--texts say about Him. So, we now have the full movement: witness, direct but mediate object, indirect but terminal object. Not every piece of biblical exegesis in the *Church Dogmatics* follows such a course; and yet while less frequent than other, more direct approaches, the logic of this type of exegesis is a prominent and familiar feature of "Barthian" exegesis.

The final outcome, once again, raises the question why the passage needs to be exegeted at all, since it yields Pauline Christology which can readily be found in Paul. Barth argues that his use of the method of typology-- our name for the relation that is sustained between the mediate and the terminal object--is intended to safeguard the full reality and historical concreteness of the figures which typify Jesus Christ. Indeed, typology is distinguished from allegory in part by just such an intention. I think that he has fulfilled such an intention; the amount of space and obvious fascination directed to the elaboration of the rituals of Lev. 14 and 16 indicates, in this instance at least, Barth's claim to let the individuality of a biblical text stand. However, one must ask why he finds this particular terminus to this passage? And why this particular terminus to so many passages? His answer is, of course, "faith in Jesus Christ" (p. 366). And when the helpfulness of this answer has been exhausted--as it soon is, surely--his answer is to challenge the reader to provide a better Christian exegesis of such a passage (p. 366). Little in the way of clarification and evaluation is possible in response to such an answer.

An indirect approach is also used by Barth in his exegesis of the David and Saul stories in the Old Testament (pp. 384-93). We have remarked above on Barth's presentation of the theme of election as he finds it in these stories. And yet the election of Saul and

David is not the terminus of these passages. *That* the texts, as they stand, point beyond themselves to an object not present in the Old Testament texts as such, is signalled in the text by the inherent inscrutability of the subject matter of these texts. Does God will a king? And which king? And how can He will both Saul and David? Furthermore, the inherent textual inscrutability is compounded in this instance by the post-textual flow of history: Israel loses its monarchy, and with it, seemingly, the condition for the possibility of these texts being meaningful at all. They are either meaningless--in which case they have only their indirect, mediate object, Saul and David, whom the flow of history has driven beyond the horizon of meaningful experience--or they are meaningful, by virtue of the fact that they point beyond themselves to their true object, Jesus Christ. This latter is of course Barth's answer.

David and Saul, individually and together, are a type of Jesus Christ. These Old Testament texts bear witness to the election of these kings of Israel, who in turn exist as figures in these stories to attest the reality of Jesus Christ. *What* they attest is again New Testament Christology. Barth finds six or seven actual points of typological comparison; however, whether consciously or not, he is repeating his own version of New Testament and Reformation Christology. The emphasis is clearly *not* on supporting the claim that Jesus Christ is present to Old Testament faith--a common apologetic thrust of much typological exegesis in the history of doctrine. Nor is the burden of this material a deepening of the church's understanding of Jesus Christ based on a Christian reading of the Old Testament; the Christological material is not that different from what Barth finds in the New Testament itself. If anything, the point seems to be the offering of evidence that every biblical text--including these Old Testament texts--

can be read Christologically. In other words, the direction of the typology is typology itself. The typology is not a means to an end, not a method, or instrument; the typology is its own end, its own goal. Jesus Christ is here too!--such is the upshot of this exegesis.

Barth's exegesis of I Kings 13 is anomalous with respect to the other pieces of exegesis in this excursus, in that Barth only indicates, but does not provide, a typological exegesis leading to the true object of the passage (pp. 408-9). He alludes to signals in the passage pointing beyond the Old Testament text as such, and indicates that the grave of the man of God and the prophet is continued in the story of the resurrection of Jesus Christ; nevertheless, for the most part he simply states *that* Jesus Christ is the true subject of this "prophetic" passage. The exegesis is thus an example of the indirect approach, though the terminus is merely stated but not depicted.

Why is this? And how is it that Barth can provide several pages--several brilliant pages, surely--of analysis of a preliminary, mediate subject matter, and devote less than a page to merely mentioning the final point, the real object, the true subject of the passage-- Jesus Christ? The oddity does at least seem to confirm that Barth is more interested in the *that* of typology than the *what.* Moreover, the anomaly seems to be explained by the fact that the New Testament-Pauline-Reformation Christology that would appear at this point has clearly been provided in his exegesis of Lev. 14 and 16, and the Saul and David stories. And this surely inclines one to suspect that the connection between primary and secondary object is tenuous at best. No matter what voice is sounded down below, the echo from above is the same dull thud--or so it seems.

We have now concluded our summary analysis of Barth's exegesis under the concept of "witness." Attention has been given to Barth's repeated attempt to find in a given biblical text its witness to the Word of God, and to following Barth in his attempt to move from that witness to its object, whether directly or indirectly. Certain questions have been raised concerning the ultimate outcome of Barth's biblical exegesis, questions which revolve around the broader issue of Christocentric interpretation of the Bible. It is to this latter issue that we turn next.

CHAPTER 2

Christ and the Bible

The most prominent characteristic of Barth's biblical exegesis in these volumes of the *Church Dogmatics* is its enormous variety. Nevertheless, *if* one is to isolate for consideration a single tendency more prominent than others it would be the tendency toward Christocentric exegesis. By "Christocentric exegesis" I here mean, most generally, the tendency to refer, in a wide variety of exegetical contexts, to Jesus Christ. How, and to what purpose, this reference is made, is the subject of our present chapter.

What we can not here give evidence of is the amount of exegesis in the *Church Dogmatics* that is *n o t* Christocentric in any suitable sense. Page after page of biblical exegesis will proceed with neither implicit nor explicit reference to Jesus Christ or Christological themes. It is not so much that these excursuses are pointedly about something else; they are simply not Christocentric. Some comments have been made in the previous chapter about the way Barth proceeds in his exegesis of biblical texts. The point I wish to make now is that Barth's approach often is, but just as often is *not*, pressed into the service of a Christocentric exegesis. And these non-Christocentric excursuses are not centered around something else; they rather are as various as the concerns of the whole Bible and the Christian universe of discourse--as appreciated by the extent of Barth's grasp.

Nevertheless, Barth tends in the *Church Dogmatics* to superimpose upon much of this variety a comprehensive exegetical unity. And this unity is uniformly centered around Jesus Christ. As Barth states it, "The object of the biblical texts is quite simply the name of Jesus Christ, and these texts can be understood only when understood as determined by this object" (I.2, p. 727). Theoretical statements of this sort--and they crop up now and again in a wide variety of contexts in Barth's theology--are useless for determining what to expect and what one finds in Barth's biblical exegesis. Indeed, it is difficult to imagine any exegesis that is remotely interesting that follows such a prescriptive statement. Fortunately, however, concern for Barth's theoretical self-description is not the focus of this study; it is sufficient to refer briefly to the fact that Barth often argued in dogmatic contexts for a Christocentric exegesis.

One further point is in order by way of introduction. The problem of Christocentric exegesis is *not* identical with the problem of the relationship between Old and New Testaments, and this because, from the point of view of Barth's exegesis (and dogmatic exposition), the New Testament is just as problematic in reference to Jesus Christ as is the Old Testament. Whatever else it is, Christocentric exegesis is not primarily *historical*; consequently, the historical, causal relationship that might be thought to subsist between the New Testament and the person of Jesus Christ not only does not solve, but does not even enter into the problem of the Christocentric shape of exegesis. The upshot of these statements is that raising the question of Christocentric exegesis does not *ipso facto* raise the question of similarities and differences in the exegesis of Old and

New Testament texts. This latter question will thus constitute a second area of analysis in this chapter, an area customarily associated with, though not in Barth logically raised by, the problem of Christocentric exegesis.

Christ and the Testaments

We begin our analysis with the similarities and differences in Barth's exegesis of the Old Testament and the New Testament, while beginning at the same time our consideration of the problem of Christocentric exegesis. The two questions are distinct but related, as we shall see. The most common form that an exegetical excursus takes in the *Church Dogmatics* is as follows. There is, firstly, an exegesis of one or more Old Testament texts raising a doctrinal point or theme. There then occurs an exegesis of one or more New Testament texts relating to that point or theme; and in this second stage of the exegesis some reference to Jesus Christ occurs. And finally, there is a summary of the theme from the biblical point of view as a whole, a summary in which the reference to Jesus Christ becomes the center of the theme under discussion. Old Testament, New Testament, Christocentric summary; such is the form of a typical piece of Barth's exegesis. For example, while discussing the knowledge of God, Barth introduces an exegetical excursus on God's "mediability"--God's will to reveal Himself through secondary signs and objects. Barth firstly discusses this theme from Old Testament texts, chiefly Ex. 33. 11-23 on the meeting of Moses and God. Then Barth discusses the New Testament theme of the Incarnation and Reconciliation as God's comprehensive "mediability" in Jesus Christ. He then concludes with a general discussion of the biblical message on God's mediability in Jesus Christ, the Messiah of Israel (Old Testament) and content of the Gospel (New Testament) (II.1, pp. 18-21). Numerous examples of this general form could be produced. Nevertheless, while statistically the norm, the above form of an excursus is hardly the only kind one finds. Many passages depart from such a form really by having no form at all; there are occasions, for example, when Barth will go back and forth between individual verses from several different books in both Testaments and include no summary whatsoever. Such departures, however, are less instructive for our purposes than those exceptions which substitute a more identifiable form for the one that we have isolated as typical. Barth will at times, for example, proceed with a discussion of a theme in each Testament and include no Christocentric summary whatsoever. For example, in support of his doctrine of the "one-sidednesses" of revelation Barth exegetes two Old Testament passages, then two New Testament themes, each of which illustrates the one-sidedness of a biblical reference to revelation. And that is the upshot of the exegetical excursus: these one-sidednesses of revelation in the Bible. No summary, and certainly no Christocentric summary, is offered; the Old Testament and New Testament are clearly thought to cohere without it (I.1, pp. 179-81). Or, Barth can provide a discrete exegesis of an Old Testament passage with no mention of the New Testament, nor of Jesus Christ. Such are, for example, the exegesis of the story of Jacob wrestling at Jabbok (I.2, pp. 338-9) and the exegesis of the meeting of Moses with God in Exodus 3 (II.1, pp. 60-1). He will similarly concentrate on a New Testament passage or passages to the exclusion of the Old, as can be seen in his exegesis of a series of Pauline passages on personal religious experience (I.2, p. 332). Finally, the customary pattern can be broken at the final stage; there can be no Christocentric summary, or there can be

a summary involving a different focal point. As evidence
of the latter, consider an excursus where Barth presents
Old and New Testament texts bearing witness to a
confusing view of the relation of God and the "space" He
occupies, only to provide the key to these texts with
the doctrine of the Trinity (II.1, pp. 474-6).

(That it is
the Trinity, and not Jesus Christ, that provides the key
to these texts, does make a difference in this context;
often enough the Christocentrism is evidently to the
exclusion of the other "persons" of the Trinity, and to
the Trinity as a separate doctrinal concern.) My point is
this: the typical form of a piece of exegesis certainly
supports a balanced concern for the exegesis of both
Testaments, while maintaining a Christocentric
reference for the whole. Nevertheless, the number and
variety of exceptions to the statistical norm insure that
the typical form itself does not guarantee automatically
a single pervasive approach to the problem of the two
Testaments, nor to the centrality of Jesus Christ in
exegesis.

Before turning directly to the question of
Christocentric exegesis, let us ask again concerning the
two Testaments as such: just what is the result of an
excursus involving both Testaments with respect to the
relative theological value of each Testament? Again,
the typical approach seems to be something like the
following. During the exegesis of the Old Testament, the
New, or the Christocentric summary, Barth will
repeatedly comment concerning both the similarities
and the differences in the Old Testament and New
Testament witness to a topic. The final weight, however,
seems to fall on the similarities, especially as
understood in a Christocentric exegetical context. The
final result, therefore, is an affirmation of both
Testaments as a relatively united witness. A good
example of this "classic" approach is an excursus in
which Barth considers the biblical witness to the idea

that God reveals Himself by going out of Himself, by being "God a second time in a very different way." The Old Testament witness, centered around the "name" of God, is surely different from the more palpable New Testament witness to the Incarnation; the Old Testament is nevertheless a pointer to the very heart of the New Testament view, and the New Testament texts themselves are engaged in a battle in defense of the Old Testament witness (I.1, pp. 316-9). Exceptions to this general rule are, however, somewhat frequent. There are times when Barth concedes no difference between the Testaments whatsoever, usually in an attempt to counter a classic Christian rejection of an Old Testament theme. Such, for example, are Barth's many exegetical excursuses on Old Testament Law, in the context of the doctrine of Gospel and Law (e.g. I.2, pp. 273-4). On the other hand, however, Barth can also find no similarities, mostly to the detriment of the Old Testament. For example, in an excursus on the life-content of the elect individual as individual, Barth finds in the Old Testament no witness whatsoever; the 30 or so pages of the excursus are then devoted entirely to exegesis of New Testament texts (II.2, pp. 419 ff.).

Less frequent, perhaps, are those occasions on which Barth argues that the Old Testament has a witness, and the New Testament has a witness, but that the New Testament simply *replaces* the Old, regardless of the range of similarities and differences. This approach occurs, for example, in an excursus in which Barth argues that certain aspects of Old Testament Law are simply replaced by New Testament sanctification (I.2, pp. 359-61). Entirely absent, on the other hand, are passages in which Barth affirms the Old Testament witness to the detriment of the New Testament. For the most part one must speak of the New Testament "supplementing" and "clarifying" the Old Testament witness, as Barth himself does in an excursus on wisdom in the Bible (II.1, pp. 432-9). Jesus Christ here represents an advance on the typologically related wisdom-figure of Solomon in the Old Testament. What can one say, in summary, concerning Barth's approach to Old and New Testament texts respectively? There is certainly no attempt absolutely to denigrate either; an approach like Marcion's is, therefore, excluded. Nor is there any evidence of the Protestant liberal historical approach to the problem of the Old Testament, whether appreciatively (Herder . . . etc.) or not (Schleiermacher . . . etc.). The categories of expectation-recollection, and promise-fulfillment exclude from the outset any such approach to the problem; there is, that is, *no moment* in the exegesis of an Old Testament passage when the text is *not* considered to be intrinsically related to the center of the Christian gospel in some fashion. Nevertheless, Barth's approach is not uniform; there are times when his heavily Christianized Old Testament is logically and formally related to medieval exegesis in one form or another. There are, on the other hand, times when the balance tips in favor of a relatively independent Old Testament witness--the characteristic of much Reformation, especially Calvinistic, exegesis. I do not think that Barth can be said to have a single view of, a single approach to, this topic. Depending on the context, he can evince widely divergent, indeed often contradictory, tendencies. Given that this topic is related to the topic of Christocentric exegesis (though not, in Barth's theology, identical), it can be concluded that Barth's approach to the two Testaments in general is insufficiently stable to provide the key to the problem of Christocentric exegesis. How it is that Jesus Christ is related to the exegesis of the Bible cannot be answered in Barth's exegesis by asking concerning the differences and similarities in his exegesis of the Old and New Testaments respectively. To recapitulate, we are concerned in this chapter with the Christocentric dimension of Barth's biblical exegesis. One possible approach to this topic is to ask concerning the exegetical treatment of Old and New Testaments; we have now tried this approach, without issue. Among other things, the point has been made that the New Testament is equally as problematic with respect to Jesus Christ as the Old; "Christocentric" exegesis is as apparent, therefore, in Barth's exegesis of the New Testament as in his exegesis of the Old.

We ask, now, concerning the precise nature of Christocentricity in Barth's biblical exegesis. How is Jesus Christ brought into relation to a biblical text? And which Jesus Christ? We turn, firstly, to the former of these questions, the question of *how*. Barth's exegetical material yields two distinct answers. Jesus Christ can be, firstly, brought into relation to a text *conceptually*; or, secondly, Christ can be brought into relation to a biblical text *personally*. Examples will make this clearer, but as a preliminary description it can be said that Barth will, on the one hand, interpret a biblical text in the light of Christological concepts, and on the other, in the light of the person/character Jesus Christ.

Christological concepts are often used to unify what is otherwise biblical diversity without a coherent logical or historical center. For example, in an exegetical excursus supporting his doctrine of the Trinity several biblical concepts and themes--God's righteousness and wisdom, God's body, God's name and covenant, the human existence of Jesus Christ--are all comprehended under the Christological concept "God a second time in a different way" (I.1, pp. 317-9). Clearly enough the Christological center unifies what is otherwise hard to conceive as inter-related conceptually or historically.

Whether the Christological reference occurs by force on the one hand, or more naturally and by persuasion on the other hand, surely depends on one's presuppositions as to the nature of exegesis. Barth clearly assumes in such a context that the absence of such a reference, such a unifying center, spells the illegitimacy of the undertaking from a theological point of view. The absence of such a center is, therefore, in Barth's eyes what is forced; and the presence what is natural and persuasive. And just as clearly such a viewpoint as Barth's is completely backward from a wide variety of viewpoints, many of them profoundly "theological." At any rate, our first point is simply that conceptual Christocentric exegesis is often unifying in tendency and tactic.

The location of this conceptual center in the strategy of an exegetical excursus can be more a controlling device which gathers and edits the biblical material, or more by way of an explanation which follows and processes it. In the case of the former a Christological concept or concepts will be used to guide the reading of one or more biblical passages from the outset. In dealing with the holiness of God, for example, Barth uses the Christological concept of the unity of judgement and grace to isolate a series of texts in both Testaments which correspond with this theme, and which are then read directly in light of it (II.1, pp. 363-7). To be sure, within, so to speak, the local exegesis of these biblical passages there can be little or no mention of Jesus Christ. Nevertheless, from the outset, and often enough throughout the exegesis and at its conclusion as well, mention is made of the fact that the unity of judgement and grace in Jesus Christ is the object which called these texts into being regardless of the diversity of their local meaning. The Holiness Code, which Barth provides with an extended local exegesis with no Christological reference, is introduced with the words: "The concrete context of the Holiness Code simply illustrates--as is necessary in the economy of revelation in expectation of Jesus Christ--this complete, all-embracing divine action for man" (p. 364). Examples of this sort abound. I distinguish them from what follows below because the Christocentric reference logically precedes the exegetical diversity.

The Christological reference can, however, more nearly follow the exegesis, as if by way of conceptual explanation for a previously established problem or puzzle. Such an approach appears just as little, or just as much, forced, depending on one's assumptions about the nature of exegesis. Barth will find in the Bible a loose end, a thread running nowhere, an anomalous passage, a conceptual absurdity, a convoluted or contradictory argument; he will then assert that Christ--i.e., in this instance a Christological concept--*explains* the conundrum, of whatever sort. A classic example of this sort is Barth's exegesis of Romans I. 18ff. in the context of a denial of a biblical basis for the concepts of natural theology (II.1, pp. 118 ff.) The passage seems to speak, Barth asserts, of a naturally acquired knowability of God by humanity in the cosmos. Such a text is anomalous with respect to other Pauline and biblical passages according to Barth; it is, or poses, a conceptual problem. The explanation of the passage, the solution to the problem, is the concept of revelation in Christ. Whatever else the text means, it *can't* mean a revelation of God independent of Jesus Christ because in the Christian universe of discourse there is none. It is, therefore, speaking of a Christologically motivated concern for the *universality* of the revelation of God in the cosmos; and notice, *in* the cosmos, not *by* the cosmos. Christological conceptual solutions of this sort recur frequently in Barth's exegesis. And just how necessary they are, in Barth's eyes, can be seen statements concerning the results of their absence. He states, for example, that apart from the Christological concept of the election of and by Jesus Christ the Bible appears downright synergistic (II.1, p. 183). Certain exegetical passages which we here name Christocentric are rather different from those we have discussed so far. Instead of a conceptual Christocentricity, these passages exhibit what can be called a *personal* Christocentricity. The difference lies in the way Jesus Christ is brought into relation to the biblical text under discussion (as well as in the identity of the Jesus Christ who is brought into this relation, as we shall see below). Personal Christocentricity corresponds roughly to what has traditionally been called typology. In both, the aim is to unify two or more discrete narrative texts into a larger narrative world embracing both, without, however, sacrificing the individual integrity of the texts. This latter qualification, of course, provides considerable room for individual judgement on the part of the reader; just when the individual texts have been lost in the larger narrative world has always been a matter of controversy, and, as the Reformation shows, can become schismatic in the extreme: Luther's first major theological production was, in his eyes, an attempt to rescue the individual integrity of the Psalter from its imposed "Christian" narrative world.[1] At any rate, I wish to point out here only that Barth uses an approach similar to traditional typology while exhibiting himself a considerable range of approaches on the relation of an individual narrative text to its larger narrated world.

With few exceptions (cf. the figure of Judas as the primary type of all sinners in the Bible, II.2, p 505) Jesus Christ is the personal center of Barth's typological exegesis of the Bible. Passage after passage of Barth's

---

[1]For this reading of Luther, see James Samuel Preuss, *From Shadow to Promise* (Cambridge: Belknap, Harvard, 1969).

biblical exegesis attempts to bring a biblical text into relation to the person of Jesus Christ. This is usually accomplished by attempting to locate the figure of Jesus Christ in, or into, a biblical text. For example, Barth calls up several biblical texts referring to "strangers" on the fringes of the biblical world, beginning with Melchisedek, and running through Balaam, Ruth, Hiram, Naaman, Cornelius, and so forth. Each of these figures, it should be pointed out, occurs in a discrete narrative context in one part of the Bible or another. Barth goes on to conclude, however, that each is a confirmatory witness of Jesus Christ. On the fringes of the biblical world stand these figures testifying, in their person and mission, to the person and mission of Jesus Christ. Out of the many of these varied biblical texts comes the One of the figure of Jesus Christ; out of several narratives, one overarching narrative, at the center of which is only one Stranger.

There is, of course, an ambiguity in the method itself, as well as in Barth's appropriation of it. Just what is the status of the individual texts when they have been typologically exegeted thus? Do they still have an independent voice? Do they "mean" anything other than their place in the larger narrative world? It appears that a more aggressive typology could be concerned to displace the individual text with the larger narrative world into which it has been placed, while a milder approach could somehow attempt to have it both ways-- have, that is, an individual text as individual text and as part of a larger whole. There is similarly an ambiguity as to just how much, if any, of the individuality of a text must be erased or blurred when it is typologically exegeted. That these issues concerned Barth, and not just as minor technical issues of exegesis but as profound theological issues as well, can be seen from one of many statements about the subject: "The name of

Jesus Christ is thus not to be regarded in any sense, open or secret, as a name for man. Neither is it to be regarded as a name for the men who stand in a definite historical connection with Jesus Christ, as forerunners or followers" (I.2, p. 12). This is a statement for a milder type of typology, not only for the sake of the integrity of the individual figure or text, but more importantly for the central type, Jesus Christ. The more completely the overarching narrative world displaces the individual narrative, and the more aggressively it does so in method, the more it appears that Jesus Christ is in fact the true reality of biblical humanity in general, or indeed of all humanity. And this conclusion--a hallmark of certain forms of protestant liberalism--Barth wished to avoid at all costs, because it can be so easily logically converted: all humanity is the true reality of Jesus Christ.

I here wish to argue that Barth's theoretical concerns were not always safeguarded by his actual exegesis. That is, Barth's exegesis exhibits a range of options on issues of this sort, many of which clearly breach the rule standing behind the theological concern as stated above. An example of a milder typology consonant with Barth's theological concern can be seen in an excursus supporting his doctrine of election in which individual elect figures from the Old Testament are related typologically to the one elect, Jesus Christ (II.2, pp. 55-8). While Jesus Christ, as the archetypal elect man, is favorably compared with each individual, careful provision is made to insist that Jesus Christ is not identical with any of these figures, nor they with him. A similar exegesis of a related topic exhibits, however, the more aggressive typology that characterizes much of Barth's exegesis (II.2, pp. 388-93). Saul and David, and the Israelite monarchy generally, are the prototype of Jesus Christ in such a way that Jesus *replaces* Saul and David as the real character of the Old Testament

David as the real character of the Old Testament
narrative material. Jesus Christ *is* Saul; Jesus Christ *is*
David. Or, as Barth states it, "The King Jesus Christ is
the true subject and hero of these stories of the kings"
(p. 391). In his exegesis of this material, therefore, the
larger narrative world *replaces* the individual texts;
and this larger narrative world has room for only *one*
character, *one* man. Saul and David disappear; these Old
Testament passages are about the King, Jesus Christ,
and *His* rule. Again, my point is this: when it comes to
personal Christocentricity, or typology, Barth can be
more aggressive or more mild in his approach; the
resulting exegesis is vastly different in each case (and
leads, in a related issue, to a vastly different theology).

A distinction similar to that considered above is a
distinction between, so to speak, two different Christs
so related to the texts of the Bible.   When Barth
interprets a biblical text Christocentrically, the Christ
applied to the text is usually either of two very
different sorts: Christ as the logical subject of
theological values in the Bible, or Christ as the narrated
subject of biblical stories.   We consider, firstly, Christ
as logical subject, and begin with a quote from Barth
which summarizes theoretically this exegetical
approach: "For them (the New Testament writers)
wisdom, righteousness, sanctification, redemption, are
not relevant conceptions in themselves, but only as
predicates of the subject Jesus" (I.2, p. 10).   Whatever
the Bible has to say of positive significance--and indeed
of negative significance as well--about almost anything
whatsoever, it is customary for Barth to attempt to
relate such theological values (Barth calls them
'predicates') to Christ as their possessor.   The Christ so
related is not so much previously defined as he is
defined in this exegetical process itself.   In other words,
unlike a narrated Christ with established and

Christ as logical subject is not so much brought to a passage as he, rather, emerges from it. Theological values are identified in a passage, and then, without changing these 'logical predicates,' Christ is asserted as their subject. Two examples, it is hoped, will make this clearer.

Consider, firstly, an excursus on "wisdom" (II.1, pp. 427-39) in which Barth expounds a short series of classical wisdom texts in Old and New Testaments. He finds a great variety of features of wisdom, but reduces the variety to an outline of three essential features: wisdom is a judge between right and wrong; wisdom is the object of acceptance and rejection; wisdom is the verdict, the decision itself concerning right and wrong. Wisdom is therefore primarily judicial and administrative. Now, Barth's final point is that Jesus Christ unites these three aspects in himself: Jesus is the wise judge, the object of decision, and the decision itself. And that is the end of the exegesis; theological values emerge from one or more biblical texts--call them biblical concepts, perhaps--and Christ is asserted as their logical subject, their possessor. In a sense this is a less aggressive form of Christocentric exegesis, in that the biblical text is left relatively undisturbed. The predicates are not in themselves altered. In another sense, however, nothing could be more aggressive, for *every* biblical predicate comes to be possessed of this one logical subject. Furthermore, the relative lack of previously established identity means that this Christ can roam freely throughout the theological values of the Bible without fear of contradiction or conflict. The predicates are not, so to speak, cumulative; with each new set of biblical concepts comes the fresh assertion that Christ is their possessor.

A second example of this sort is Barth's long exegesis of the Sermon on the Mount (II.2, pp. 683-700). The most important point Barth makes, exegetically, is his assertion that the Sermon on the Mount is only incidentally about obedience and disobedience, or the life of the Christian, but is really about the coming of the kingdom, the new man, in Jesus Christ. In other words, the Sermon on the Mount is not about the Christian but about Christ. Just how this takes place involves a complicated series of attempts to translate each imperative of the Sermon into a Christological statement: to attach, in our language, each theological value to its logical subject, Jesus Christ.

The second answer to the question of the identity of Jesus Christ in the Christocentric exegesis of the Bible offered by Barth's exegesis is Christ as *narrated subject*. The Christ which Barth brings into relation to a biblical text, Old Testament or New, is the Christ narrated in the Gospels; Jesus Christ, that is, as the subject of those acts whose rough contours in the Gospels (birth, life, death, resurrection . . . etc.) make up a literary character. No particular moment in the literary depiction of this character is given exclusive exegetical rights by Barth; that is, it is not only the crucified Christ, or the resurrected Christ, or the Christ which is the transition between the two, or any other moment which is used as *the* nodal point in Christ's story to unlock the meaning of other biblical texts. Usually a pattern of some sort will be found in the biblical texts under discussion--more often than not a narrative pattern of some sort. Barth will then argue that the narrative pattern is isomorphic with a pattern in the story of Jesus. He will then conclude that the biblical text under discussion finds its ultimate interpretive context by being associated with the story of Jesus in one or more of its features. The narrated Christ is thus the key which unlocks the mystery of these texts.

One of the most common examples of this sort of exegesis is an exegetical association between Yahweh as an agent in the Old Testament and the story of Jesus as the ultimate interpretive context for these texts. For example, Barth relates the many places in which Yahweh *sends* his representatives in the Old Testament to the New Testament stories of Jesus *sending* his disciples (I.2, pp. 490-1); a pattern in the Old Testament is brought into relation with a pattern in the story of Jesus which acts as the interpretive context for the whole. In this case the figure of Jesus does not replace, or even diminish, the figure of Yahweh in the Old Testament. An exegetical association is established, and while the direction of the flow of interpretation is clear--the passages of this sort always conclude by talking about Jesus, never about Yahweh--a rough balance is maintained between primary type and secondary type. Barth can also, though only infrequently, pursue a more aggressive typology between Yahweh and Jesus, in which Jesus replaces Yahweh as the agent of Old Testament occurrences (cf. II.1, p. 420).

Another example of this sort of exegesis is the typology we have previously examined between David and Saul, the kings of Israel, and Jesus Christ (II.2, pp. 389-93). In this instance, a series of patterns in the Old Testament portrayal of these kings is stated by Barth to be isomorphic with a series of patterns in the story of Jesus. The stories are thus ultimately a confirmation of the general contours of the story of Jesus; the characters of Saul and David lose their identity, or perhaps find their identity by being merged completely with the character Jesus Christ. The emphasis is not upon promise and fulfillment or the like; the sheer isomorphism of the literary patterns is apparently an end in itself. The story of Jesus finds this echo in the stories of these only apparently different figures in the

Bible. Barth hears this echo and reports what he finds: the story of Jesus can be found here also.

Finally, though customarily an attempt to relate two or more *narrative* passages, the narrated subject Jesus Christ can be brought into relation to a non-narrative text also. For example, Old and New Testament imperatives are asserted to be based, universally, on the indicative of the story of Jesus (II.2, p. 562). Thus, in the case of any individual Old and New Testament law or norm, the text is to be brought into relation to the story of Jesus as its ultimate basis and meaning. This approach is confirmed, for example, when in his exegesis of the Sermon on the Mount Barth argues that it is only about Christ, not about the Christian or the Christian life (II.2, pp. 687-700). Such a counter-intuitive reading of the Sermon on the Mount is more understandable when one realizes that Barth is forced by his approach to passages of this sort to bring them, whatever their content, into relation to the story of Jesus. In other words, even non-narrative elements in the story of Jesus (the Sermon, though an episode, is apparently too much a Sermon for Barth and not enough a series of acts) must be brought into relation to the story of Jesus.

Example B: The Rich Young Ruler

We turn now to the second in our series of examples from Barth's exegesis for close analysis. For the purposes of this chapter on Christocentric exegesis we have selected for analysis Barth's exegesis of the story of the Rich Young Ruler. For the convenience of the reader, there follows the text of the story as it appears in its Markan form (Mark 10. 17-31)--the form upon which Barth's exegesis concentrates:

17 And as he was setting out on his journey, a man ran up and knelt before him, and asked him, "Good Teacher, what must I do to inherit eternal life?" 18 And Jesus said to him, "Why do you call me good? No one is good but God alone. 19 You know the commandments: 'Do not kill, Do not commit adultery, Do not steal, Do not bear false witness, Do not defraud, Honor your father and mother.'" 20 And he said to him, "Teacher, all these I have observed from my youth." 21 And Jesus looking upon him loved him, and said to him, "You lack one thing; go, sell what you have, and give to the poor, and you will have treasure in heaven; and come, follow me." 22 At that saying his countenance fell, and he went away sorrowful; for he had great possessions. 23 And Jesus looked around and said to his disciples, "How hard it will be for those who have riches to enter the kingdom of God!" 24 And the disciples were amazed at his words. But Jesus said to them again, "Children, how hard it is to enter the kingdom of God! It is easier for a camel to go through the eye of a needle than for a rich man to enter the kingdom of God." 26 And they were exceedingly astonished, and said to him, "Then who can be saved?" Jesus looked at them and said, "With men it is impossible, but not with God." 28 Peter began to say to him, "Lo, we have left everything and followed you." 29 Jesus said, "Truly, I say to you, there is no one who has left home or brothers or sisters or mother or father or children or lands, for my sake and for the gospel, 30 who will not receive a hundredfold now in this time, houses and brothers and sisters and mothers and children and lands, with persecutions, and in the age to come eternal life. 31 But many that are first will be last, and the last first."

Barth's exegesis of the story of the Rich Young Ruler exhibits a rich variety of techniques of explication, to which we shall give some attention; a full treatment of the techniques of explication will be delayed, however, until our final chapter on explication. For the present, our concern is to show ways in which Barth's exegesis is *Christologically* motivated and informed. And for this purpose, his exegesis of the story of the Rich Young Ruler is exemplary, in that it displays a variety of ways of making what is ultimately one, simpleminded, concentrated, exegetical move: bringing Jesus Christ into relation to a biblical text. The fact that it is a New Testament text, and indeed a narrative from the larger narrative of Jesus Christ, will serve to stress that the problems of Christocentric exegesis are by no means unique to the Old Testament.

The exegesis of the story of the Rich Young Ruler occurs in Barth's treatment of theological ethics in the doctrine of God (II.2, pp. 613-30). The precise doctrinal issue under discussion is the form and nature of the divine command as *claim*, and the major point that Barth makes theologically is that this divine claim is constituted, through and through, by its relation to the person of Jesus Christ. This latter point--the Christological form of the divine claim--is the immediate doctrinal context for the exegetical excursus on the Rich Young Ruler, to which we now turn.

We shall begin our analysis with a consideration of the initial exchange between Christ and the rich young ruler (vv. 17-20) as it appears in Barth's exegesis. He "ran up and knelt before him"; right away, with his exposition of this clause, Barth's Christological expansion of the passage becomes evident. In kneeling before Jesus, Barth argues, the inquirer bears witness to the *objective validity* of Christ's reign, for him, even as disobedient, as well as for all others, including of course the obedient. The action of the passage thus takes place in the context of the ruling power of Jesus Christ in His Kingdom, the Kingdom of God. The man adjusts himself to this rule; he acknowledges, that is, that Christ's rule is true for him precisely in his disobedience. Furthermore, by asking Jesus the question concerning eternal life, the man also attests that Jesus, and Jesus alone, can answer the question concerning the content of hope;   "for it is in Jesus that there has been concluded between God and man the covenant which forms the beginning of all the ways and works of God, and therefore the objective law under which the existence of all living creatures runs its course" (p. 613).

What might be considered a religious-ethical situation involving decision has been converted by expanding Christological exegesis into a *juridical* situation between a king and his servant, in which the fundamental relation is not decision but objectively valid rule and presence. Signals for the expansion and conversion are there in the text: he knelt, and asked *Jesus* the question. Few would agree, however, that the signals are unambiguous, and many would argue-- including most traditional Christian exegesis of this passage--that they point off in a different direction altogether.   And yet, for Barth the expansion and conversion seem natural and complete, and are offered undefended and even unsupported.

Jesus' initial response-why call me good?--Barth considers an unambiguous self-reference to His own divine rule.   The character Jesus thus confirms the Christological cast of the story as a whole by referring to His own sole rule, His own power and prerogative to give His commanding Word in such a way that no response is left open but obedience or disobedience. Jesus has decided, Barth argues, to *reveal* the customarily *concealed* reality of His Divine Word and Will to this man, as confirmed by the fact that the man approaches Him in the way that he does.   The story is thus a revelatory-juridical situation; the man has come to solicit a judicial response--i.e. a response of condemnation or approval, as opposed to a response of ethical or religious advice--from the man in whom God's own Word is directly present and apprehensible.   Jesus is not just a *character* in the story; the rule of Jesus Christ over all is the *setting* for the story.   The characters and exchanges in the story *conform* to this setting, but they do not *generate* it. Jesus responds with a reference to the commandments. According to Barth, this response is already a complete and devastating judgement against the man, only in a concealed form. Such a reading certainly conforms to the larger Christological setting which Barth has given the story, but even signals, hints, that the reference to the commandments spells wholesale condemnation seem absent from the text. Furthermore, that Jesus refers to the commandments means for Barth a backward reference to the previously established relationship between Jesus and the man; that is, a reference to the objectively valid rule of Christ through the Will of God expressed in the Old Testament. As Barth glosses this reference:

> Therefore when He answers the questioner, in principle and substance He can only repeat what He has already said to him. That is just what He does when He refers him to the commands. He has already told him what he should do to inherit eternal life. Therefore the questioner knows very well what should be the form of life of one who has this prospect, claim and hope. It is not for nothing that he was in the kingdom of Jesus Christ even before he came to Him. (p. 615)

Jesus continues with a brief enumeration of certain commands; according to Barth these are all from the "second table" of the Law, and represent the external, concrete, doing or not doing side as opposed to the internal side of loving and fearing God above all things. The former relate to the treatment of our neighbor, the latter to our inward relation to God. The former are, furthermore, evidence of the latter. Now, according to Barth, Jesus refers to the second table in order to posit

Himself as the man's neighbor. In other words, how he relates to *this* Neighbor, how he fulfills in relation to *this* Person the concrete demands of the Law, will give evidence, indeed will determine, whether or not he loves God, and in so doing has eternal life. To quote Barth: "'You know the commandments'--how they are given you in the sphere of the most concrete doing or not doing, in dealings with your fellow man. It is in this sphere that you meet them again, now that you confront your neighbor in Me and My person" (p. 616). The character Jesus, of course, does not say this, nor anything remotely like it. But the character Jesus, understood in the setting of His Divine and Kingly rule, can only mean this by what is said--or so Barth argues. Even narratives about Jesus must be Christologically interpreted.

In the final moment of the initial exchange, the rich young ruler affirms his obedience. Barth sees in this affirmation complete disobedience, in the form of an attempt to justify himself before God his Judge. His answer is secretly rebellion--secret, that is, from himself, but not from the reader, who can apparently see in his answer only rebellion. Barth argues that the man has only related himself to the external side of the Law, never to the internal. He, he *himself*, does not *belong* to Jesus; he recognizes the objective validity of his kingdom, and yet rebels from inwardly embracing the King Himself. Nevertheless, this rebellion is concealed in his answer, and will only be brought to light as the story proceeds. Notice that the expansion is, in this instance, entirely "psychological" in nature; the spaces which Barth fills in are the interior spaces of the character in the story, about which the actual narrator of the story gives, in this instance, no information or clue.

There follows the sequel to the initial exchange between Jesus and the rich young ruler. Barth considers it "astonishing" that we do not hear abject condemnation from the mouth of Jesus. Barth is astonished, of course, because he considers the rich young ruler to have openly and completely rebelled against God--Barth even takes to calling him "the disobedient one" throughout the remainder of the exegesis. The text states, instead of condemnation, that Jesus loved the man; Barth of course glosses this as divine, unconditional love for the disobedient and rebellious, and reasserts that the "covenant" which Christ has established with this man pre-dates, and will certainly endure beyond, the temporal scope of the story, regardless of the man's decision. Once again, a conversion has taken place in which a discrete narrative item has been converted into the non-temporal, conceptual setting for the story. God's great love for sinners is what is meant; not, or not only, Jesus' individual love for this individual man at this moment in narrated time.

Jesus loves, and then commands. But Barth converts what might be called the speech-act of "commanding" into the speech-act of "judging." Jesus does not command the man, he pronounces sentence. But why this particular conversion? Clearly enough, it conforms with the way Barth conceives God in Jesus as relating to every person, and to each person. Every "Word" of God is grace and judgement, judgement and grace--and present in the person of Jesus Christ. Thus, what the text offers as the narrative action of commanding must be put into the setting of the Jesus Christ of mercy and judgement; Jesus never just "commands." By offering the commands Jesus binds *Himself* to this man, and unveils the man's essential rebelliousness. By offering the command, Jesus makes clear to the man that "what God has already done for him belongs to him and will accrue to his benefit if he will only make use of it" (p. 619). This general attempt to establish a covenant relation with the man is the real purpose of Jesus' Word. Nevertheless, such a general principle must become concrete: "He is not the covenant-partner of God. He

does not love his neighbor.   He does not belong to Jesus.
This is what he lacks.   But it is not described in an
abstract and academic way.   It is aimed concretely at his
specific existence and condition" (p. 618).   Thus, the
command to go and sell, and follow Christ, is a particular
instance of the general principle--whose narrative
begins with time itself, or before time--of God's grace
and judgement on all humankind.   Barth apparently
perceives this principle in the concrete situation of the
text--and in his exegesis makes use of the general
principle, the general situation, the general relation.
Even the particular character Jesus in this particular
situation must be Christologically interpreted to
conform with the identity of Jesus Christ in the one,
universal, narrated--or is it any longer narrated?--
world that is God's relation to humanity.

Jesus' commands are three.   Of the first command, to
sell what he has, Barth says: "The aim of Jesus'
requirement that the rich man should divest himself of
his wealth is plain to see" (p. 620).   Notice first of all
that the command has an "aim," a something else besides
itself to explain it.   And according to Barth this aim is
freedom to be the "covenant-partner" of God, freedom
for love to God, freedom to fulfill the "first table" of the
Law and in so doing truly fulfill the "second table."   Jesus'
command takes the form that it does in order to stress
that the man has as a competing Lord with the true God
the false God Mammon, and this false God he must flee.
He must sell what he has, and in so doing be freed for the
internal side of the Law, the love of God through Jesus.

He must sell, and give all to the poor, in order to have
treasure in Heaven.   Barth states that in giving this
command Jesus instructs the man as to the *true*
meaning of the second table of the Law.   To follow God's
will is to *imitate* God, and in so doing, to bear witness
to him.   The command to give to the poor is a command

to testify to God by doing for others what He has already done for us in Christ: to give all. And indeed, according to Barth the man "sees" that in this command to give away his own is the substance and aim of all the commands. This is the one Command, the aim of all others. The man is now confronted with, and sees, the point of it all.

And finally, there is the command to follow Jesus. Barth explicates this final command as the summary of all that has preceded, and indeed the summary of all the Gospel and Law. *Jesus* is the God by whom we must be freed and whom we must love and fear above all things. *Jesus* is therefore the first table of the Law. And *Jesus* is the neighbor for whom we must be free, whom we must love as God's witness. *Jesus* is therefore the second table of the Law. Thus, all the "theological values" of the text are brought together by Barth to this one Subject. Only the character of the man is left relatively independent of this one Subject. And even of him Barth argues that what Jesus offers him is *participation* in Christ's own freedom. The command to follow Christ is the command to abandon his own "self-movement" in favor of Christ's future, and future responsibility for him.

This stage of the story closes with the statement that the man went away sorrowful. Barth stresses that his action is a *confirmation* of a previous act of condemnation by God; it is not, that is, an *enactment* of his disobedience, so much as a human echo of a *divine* act of *judgement*--i.e., Christ's judgement. The effect of Barth's exegesis is to displace the emphasis on the man's decision on to God's previously established relation to him. The man does not really *decide* anything, he merely *confirms*. And once again Barth goes on to stress that the text is not to be read as closing the door against the man; Christ's offer of grace will follow him wherever he goes. Again, the man's decision--he simply walks away--is sublimated in favor of Christ's (non-narrated, perpetual) action toward him. From beginning to end, this first section of the story is read against the backdrop of Jesus Christ's relation to all people and to each person. While it is not the major interest of this study, it should be noted that the direction of the interpretation is uniformly *away from* the narrated form of the text, and toward a perpetual relation which, if it can be narrated at all, certainly crowds out those very features of our text which make *it* a narrative.

The exchange between Christ and the rich young ruler is followed by a complementary exchange between Christ and the disciples, which in turn is divided into a discussion between Christ and the disciples as a whole and Christ and Peter in particular. We consider first Barth's exegesis of the initial discussion between Christ and the disciples (vv. 23-29). Barth certainly reads the relation of the text about the ruler and the text about the disciples as a *contrast*; he nevertheless asserts that the explanation of the contrast lies entirely in the Word of God--the command which Jesus is and speaks-- and not in the human response. It is the Word of God alone which kills and makes alive, and in the case of the disciples it has blessed, and not cursed--or so it seems initially. Barth offers this understanding based on the textual statement that Jesus "looked at them" (v. 23, 27). According to Barth, this "looking" expresses the full relation of Christ to the disciples, the very relation that is absent in the case of the rich young ruler. Nevertheless, affirms Barth, the Word of God is ultimately one, not two, and therefore in "looking" at the disciples, Jesus was looking past them to the man walking away sorrowful; he was continuing to offer him grace. And similarly, his relation to the disciples was, as we shall see, also one of judgement. Notice again that a piece of narrative ("he looked at them") is converted into a seemingly non-narrative general relation, and the particular character of Jesus assumes a comprehensive, explanatory identity.

The interchange takes place between Jesus and the disciples about who can be saved. Barth offers first an exegesis of the disciples response ("who then can be saved?" . . . etc.) and then an exegesis of Christ's words ("With men it is impossible, but not with God" . . . etc.). According to Barth, the disciples, in expressing amazement and astonishment at the words of Christ, are ranging themselves with the disobedient rich young ruler. They are confessing their own sin and rebellion. They realize, through the exchange between the man and Jesus, and through Jesus' words about it, that it is the *word of Jesus* which determines all, and not they themselves. Says Barth of the inward realization of the disciples: "In relation to Jesus, in relation to the command of God, they are in exactly the same position as this man" (p. 624).

Now, Jesus' words concerning the one way of salvation amount, according to Barth, to something like this. Human beings, whether obedient or disobedient, have *no freedom* for God. What comes to them as divine possibility is the *freedom of Jesus Christ Himself.* In other words, what comes to them is the freedom of this *other.* And what takes place in the divine possibility is that this freedom of this other is *attributed* to them as their own. Their response is simply to believe this attribution. Faith in the freedom of this other for God is their obedience, their way, their salvation. They do not become Jesus, but they become new people, other people than they are, by seeing their identity in the identity of Jesus, their freedom in the freedom of Jesus, their life in the life of Jesus. What did they do? "They accepted it as true that Jesus was obedient for them" (p. 626). Or, "they believed, i.e., they were pleased to have

His ability attributed to them, to have their own inability covered over by His ability" (p. 626).   Now, it seems clear that the figure of Jesus has exploded beyond the bounds of the story into a cosmic, vicarious redeemer of humanity, a character upon whom is cast whatsoever the story says about anybody--including the obedience of the disciples.   At best, the specific contours of the individual text seem lost in Barth's version of the generalizable relation of Jesus Christ and humanity.   And yet, the individual features are not lost, not ignored.   The text is given an exegetical setting, a setting ("Christ's relation to persons") which Barth nowhere speaks of as such.   But it is the text which is exegeted in this setting; and it is clear that Barth considers the text and the setting as ultimately conforming to one another.

The disciples, according to Barth, realize at this point that their life in faith is ultimately a call to witness. Their obedience is to bear witness to others of the obedience of Christ available to them.   For example, they realize that their mission to the rich young ruler is to proclaim to him salvation through faith in Jesus Christ alone.   Now, this aspect of the "story" is expounded by Barth with the complete absence of reference to the biblical text.   It certainly follows from all that he has said before; to attest to others the salvation that is available would naturally follow as the one call to obedience in the light of Barth's description of that salvation.   Nevertheless, Barth's depiction of the disciples' realization of this fact, this task, is not referred to any biblical text; nor, so far as I can see, can one be specified.   Apparently one thus has a kind of extrapolated exegesis in which the narrative is continued beyond its textual bounds, based on the reader's perception of the natural flow of the narrative in the text.   At any rate, Barth rarely does this kind of extrapolated narrative exegesis, and it seems clear that he is mistakenly exegeting the conceptual setting that he has given the story rather than the story itself. We conclude, now, our consideration of this exegetical excursus with an analysis of Barth's exegesis of the final exchange between Jesus and Peter (vv. 28-31). Barth begins his presentation with the final verse: "But many that are first will be last, and the last first." Two separate points are, according to Barth, communicated in this saying of Jesus. There is, firstly, the point that the "command" of Jesus--presumably the various imperatives throughout the story--is blessing and curse, curse and blessing to both the rich young ruler and the disciples. Though blessing is absent from the narrative action of Jesus toward the man, and curse is absent from his action toward the disciples, Barth concludes from Jesus' saying (and from the setting that Barth gives the story) that each *must* be present; Jesus does bless the man, and condemn the disciples--only the reader can't see it as a piece of narrative action. This is the kind of witness that we have here called *concealed*; concealed within one narrative action is really the co-presence of another. And Jesus' saying is, according to Barth, a kind of confirmation that Barth's assertion of these concealed actions is valid and necessary. It is secondly, however, a statement that the relation between Jesus and the rich young ruler on the one hand, and the disciples on the other, can be easily and quickly reversed: the disciples can become the disobedient ones, the man the obedient. The two groups are two points in a series--first and last--not two different classes or sets. They are therefore vulnerable to complete role-reversal.

Barth expounds the remainder of the exchange between Peter and Jesus on the basis of his reading of the final verse. When Peter asserts that the disciples

in complete, utter, sinful, rebellion against Christ and His
Kingdom. Such a saying is the very epitome of
disobedience. Again, the depravity of Peter's response
is *concealed* in the seemingly appropriate narrative
depiction of the actual biblical text; the evangelist does
not censure the remark, nor does the character Jesus.
But Barth claims that the remark unveils an attitude of
faithless, anxious concern for the past rather than
openness to Christ's future. And of course, Barth's
reading of Peter's statement leads naturally into his
reading of Christ's response. Concealed in Christ's
seemingly innocent promise of earthly and eternal
reward is total judgement against the disciples. It really
is concealed; there is no hint of it whatsoever in the
actual narrative depiction of Jesus' response.
Nevertheless, it is there. And not only is judgement
present in the innocent promise, but so also is the final
and ultimate promise itself: Christ Himself. In saying
what He says, according to Barth, Jesus also offers to
the disciples the true Promise concealed in every
promise: that Jesus' freedom, Jesus' obedience, Jesus'
death, Jesus' life, Jesus' *identity*, will become theirs.
Once again, the person of Jesus Christ *must* become
attached, according to Barth, to every positive value
offered up by any biblical text, even a positive value
already attached to Jesus as a character in the text.
Jesus can't just *make* a promise; he must *be* that
promise. The disciples can't *respond* to a promise;
Jesus must be the response to the promise which He
Himself is and makes. Once again, the narrative detail
and flow, even that involving Jesus as a character, has
seemingly been submerged into the one explanatory
framework for all biblical stories.[2]
    Barth concludes his analysis of the entire story of the
Rich Young Ruler with a repetition of the point that the

---

[2]If there is only one Story in the universe, is it really still a
story? How is it to be distinguished from a general condition?

promise is still extended to, and will always follow, this rebellious man. He may walk away sorrowful, but what is really important is that Jesus will always be walking after him. Barth's conclusion is, once again, clearly an attempt to render the fuller meaning of the story based on the larger conceptual setting which he gives it. We have concentrated in this chapter, and in our analysis of the exegetical example, on the part played by Jesus Christ in Barth's exegesis of the Bible. We now turn from this specific though pervasive exegetical technique to the more general, more formal problem of the presence in Barth's exegesis of the Bible of concerns from the broader framework of his dogmatic theology.

CHAPTER 3

The Bible and Theology

The exegetical corpus with which we are here concerned occurs in the context of a presentation and analysis of Christian doctrine and theology. In some quarters, of course, this fact itself would disqualify what we are studying from the name exegesis. The legacy of Enlightenment biblical criticism, rational theology, Protestant-Catholic polemic and other factors, the suspicion that theology and exegesis never truly meet is held both by those that think that exegesis is all the better for it, and by those that think likewise of theology. Whatever else it is, the *Church Dogmatics* is a direct assault on this bifurcation. It is a comprehensive presentation of Christian theology, and yet contains, in conceptual interdependency with the doctrinal presentation, hundreds of pages of biblical exegesis.

It cannot be the purpose of this study to inquire, in global terms, whether or not there is indeed a mutual fit between exegesis and doctrinal presentation in the *Church Dogmatics*. It is questionable, indeed, whether such a question is meaningful or useful in the absence of a renewed attempt to offer a similar engagement between extended biblical exegesis and theological presentation. At any rate, this general topic must here be treated in a more limited way.

I propose to consider and analyze, in this chapter, the presence of theological *pressures* on Barth's biblical exegesis. I shall not be concerned to ask what in Barth's biblical exegesis is more properly "biblical" and what "theological"--such is the global approach to the topic which I reject. Nor shall I frame the question in the insufficiently specific, insufficiently nuanced way of asking concerning "Barthian theology" in the exegesis. I ask, rather, concerning pressures, signs that the exegesis, though rather straightforward in many respects, is nonetheless the exegesis of a Christian theologian in the context of a presentation of Christian theology. In asking concerning 'signs,' 'pressures,' I assume perhaps that there is something else there in the exegesis *besides* the theologian--a counter-pressure, at the least, from the biblical text itself. Such an assumption I here make undefended, and offer it only as a useful heuristic device in tracing the special contours of Barth's distinctive way of reading the Bible.

Just how is Barth the theologian present in the exegesis of biblical texts?   A revealing example of Barth's self-conception on this topic occurs in the preface to II.2, where Barth is constrained to reflect on the seemingly radical departure of his doctrine of election from classical Christian tradition: "As I let the Bible itself speak to me on these matters, as I meditated upon what I seemed to hear, I was driven irresistibly to reconstruction" (p. X).   It all seems so simple!   But of course volumes have been written on the hermeneutic implied in such a statement.   It is not my purpose to judge concerning the validity, or indeed the possibility, of such a self-conception as Barth's. Assuming, for the sake of analysis, that there is something else in Barth's biblical exegesis besides Barth the theologian, we ask in this chapter concerning theological pressures on his reading of biblical texts, pressures due to the fact that it is *Karl Barth*, and indeed Karl Barth the *theologian*, who is 'letting the Bible itself speak to him on these matters.'

We shall consider, firstly, pressures from Barth's theological concerns broadly conceived. Attention will then be given to pressures on the biblical exegesis from Barth's appropriation of classical Christian theological language. And finally, the question will be raised concerning pressures exerted on one biblical text by Barth's reading of another biblical text--the case of so-called "parallel passages."

Exegesis as Conceptual Analysis

The most obvious, most pervasive way in which Barth's biblical exegesis is influenced by his theological approach and concerns is his tendency to expound biblical passages in terms of the "concepts" they yield. Whatever the biblical text--whatever its formal, literary features, its place in the biblical corpus, etc.--, and whatever the doctrinal issue under discussion, the aim and method of much of Barth's biblical exegesis is the analysis of biblical "concepts." More often than not, of course, the biblical-exegetical concepts are isomorphic with doctrinal concepts under discussion in the theological text. A good example--among hundreds of others--of what we have in mind here is a small series of excursuses in I.2 on the church as the Body of Christ (pp. 215-20). Several New Testament passages are said to yield a concept of the Church as the Body of Christ in which four points are present: the church is an extension of the Incarnation, the church is therefore not autonomous from its Head, nor is it divisible, and it is visibly real. This particular example of conceptual analysis is not necessarily so unusual in comparison with other approaches to the New Testament, historical and otherwise. Nevertheless, what is unusual, and characteristic of Barth, is the extent to which hundreds and hundreds of such biblical "concepts" provide the content for hundreds and hundreds of pages of biblical exegesis. Why concepts? And just what is a concept in Barth's sense? The answer to both these questions lies, I think, in Barth's understanding of the task of theology as a whole. Barth appropriated the loci-method in theology, a method which had its origins in early medieval scholasticism, and came to full fruition--in Barth's eyes at least--with early Protestant orthodoxy, only to suffer precipitous decline and demise at the hands of pietism and rationalism. Within this method, and within Barth's appropriation of it, the architechtonic of theology consists in an ordered series of loci, chapters, paragraphs, sections, and sub-sections in which the fundamental unit of discourse is the theological concept. In Protestantism especially, the theological concept is logically and materially derived from the "point," or series of points, in a *sermon*, which is in turn based on the kerygmatic intention of the biblical text. Thus, biblical text, church mission, and technical theology, while employing different rhetorics, all share a series of fundamental meaningful units of Christian discourse called in technical theology "concepts." More detailed analysis of this approach cannot be provided in this context; the concern I have is to show the *effect* of such a method on Barth's reading of biblical texts. And that effect is, most generally, a pervasive assumption that no matter what the biblical text being exegeted, it naturally and convincingly feeds into theological argument by yielding conceptual content, and conceptual clarification, for a doctrinal point under discussion. Barth never defends this approach, nor even makes it clear; the mutual fit of biblical text (kerygmatic intention, which we have previously called "witness") church mission (especially the Christian sermon) and dogmatic theology (the scientific articulation and testing of the content of text and sermon) is a real presupposition: a condition of the possibility of the project of the *Church Dogmatics* as a whole.

Whether or not Barth's way of exegeting the Bible as a supplier and judge of theological concepts is appropriate to the Bible itself is beyond the scope of this study to determine. Nevertheless, it is important at least to illustrate the full range of nearness to, and distance from, the biblical text in Barth's conceptual, exegetical analysis. What follows are two examples illustrating the limits of this range; in offering them as examples I do, of course, presuppose a judgement concerning what is near to, and what far from, the Bible. The purpose of introducing these examples is not to articulate or substantiate such a judgement, but rather to offer at least an impression of the limits of Barth's approach.[1]

As an example of what one must surely consider the felicitousness, the biblical and theological richness, of Barth's approach, consider an excursus from II.2 (pp. 597-601). The immediate doctrinal context is Barth's explication of the command of God in theological ethics

---

[1] The reader will perhaps appreciate an analogy. In the philosophical linguistic analysis of ordinary language some conceptual reconstructions seem apt, while others do not. Surely one important reason why the analysis will at times fail is the presence of extraneous, overriding philosophical commitments; the conceptual analysis, rather than *rendering* ordinary language, seems rather to *lecture* at it. The integrity of the ordinary language is lost. So also, in Barth's biblical exegesis, is there a similar scale of success (and for similar reasons) in his conceptual analysis of biblical texts; it is our purpose now to illustrate this scale.

as a command which frees human persons by giving them freedom to live, permission to live. In support of his view that the divine command is at the same time absolutely imperious and yet humbly liberating Barth offers an exegesis of several biblical passages exhibiting two opposite pairs of concepts: anxiety and fear on the one hand, and standing and abiding on the other. We will here consider only his analysis of anxiety and fear. For his analysis of fear and anxiety Barth simply quotes a string of passages from virtually every part of the New Testament. He then offers his analysis. Anxiety, he contends, is "in a sense the term for a little fear" (p. 598), in that anxiety has to do with penultimate matters which we envision, matters having to do with the life we live, and the future towards which we are moving. The anxious person is ultimately facing the question of the security of one's life. Fear, however, concerns ultimate things, indeed concerns Jesus Christ Himself. The one who is genuinely afraid is the one who is face to face with God in Jesus Christ, who has passed beyond anxiety in response to the insecurities of life and reached the shock of recognition that life itself is entirely problematic. And, Barth continues, for the New Testament this fear is equivalent to standing before God in Jesus Christ; He and He alone is the true object of fear. (It will perhaps not go unnoticed how very different is this analysis from the familiar analysis of existentialism).

Now, I have only been able to give the barest indication of Barth's analysis; the full excursus is at the same time more subtle, more supple, and yet also more definite and precise than I can here represent. But notice what emerges from my presentation. Several passages, from several layers of New Testament tradition, having several forms of New Testament literature (narrative, paranesis, apocalyptic) are all related by sharing together and exhibiting a definable, analyzable, theologically useful conceptual usage: the concepts of fear and anxiety. I consider this example felicitous because of how close it seems to the biblical text, how much it allows the reader to *notice* and *understand* at least part of what these texts have to offer to the person who is concerned with them in a setting like Barth's. It is an exegesis which is, *mirabile dictu*, at the same time true to the biblical text and yet theologically useful. Needless to say, since the rise of modern forms of biblical study and religious discourse, since, say, a Johann Salomo Semler, one is sceptical of any such claim to leap the chasm between these two disciplines. And Barth's use of theological-biblical concepts in biblical exegesis can be, and indeed has been, criticized as fundamentally a form of "dogmatic" exegesis. One must surely conclude, however, that *if* some form of conceptual analysis is appropriate to the "biblical" (as opposed to "theological") study of the Bible (and I am here thinking not primarily of the *Theological Dictionary of the New Testament* but of brilliant historical works like Bultmann's *Theology of the New Testament* with its extended passages of conceptual analysis) then Barth's must be included among the most successful examples of this sort, and precisely from the point of view of the integrity of the biblical text itself.

Nevertheless, the worst fears of the rational, historical-critical criticism of dogmatic exegesis can also be realized in reading Barth's exegesis. I do not mean to suggest that any sample can be looked at in two different ways, either positively or negatively. This too, is true; but I am rather concerned to argue that there is a range of success in Barth's ability to use his approach to illuminate rather than obscure the biblical text. As an example of where the approach fails, consider a short

series of excususes in II.1 (pp. 13-21).   The context is
Barth's presentation of his understanding of the concept
of the knowledge of God, an understanding which Barth
derived from a vigorous appropriation of the medieval
realism of Anselm of Canterbury.   Barth alludes to
several passages in the Bible where he finds the basic
thrust of his doctrine that God is an "object of
knowledge" for man the "subject," though only through
the "mediation of a secondary object." Now, I do not wish
to argue that such a conception is *necessarily*
inappropriate to the Bible, though these hardly sound
like *biblical* concepts.   I do, however, think that for
most readers of the biblical text this example from
Barth will strike them as having little to do with the
biblical text *per se*, and much more to do with Barth's
theological concerns.   Here, Barth's approach seems to
fail; conceptual analysis of the biblical text has
purchased usefulness for theology at the price of loss of
the integrity of the Bible.   Again, I am here merely trying
to illustrate the other, less successful extreme of the
range of success in Barth's conceptual reading of the
Bible.   While there are times when Barth's analysis seems
to cause the reader to notice what is there in the Bible
as if for the first time, there are other times when his
analysis is distant from the biblical text, when most
readers will, I think, turn away disappointed at how little
of the Bible has been made clear, at how much has been
obscured.   Such a dialectic between success and failure
is perhaps true of every expositor of the Bible, though
Barth's successes do seem so very brilliant, his failures
so very unfortunate.   But the point I am here stressing is
that the reason for this dialectic in Barth lies in part in
the method that he adopted in doing biblical exegesis as
a theologian.   Finding theological concepts in the Bible,
as a method, does not determine whether or not Barth is
a good or bad exegete;   but it is, at one and the same

time, the instrument both for his brilliant successes and his disappointing failures.

The conceptual-analytical method that Barth uses in his exegesis insures at least the appearance of a natural fit between dogmatic exposition and biblical exegesis. They are rarely in tension, and are almost always mutually supportive, mutually confirming. It is the biblical exegesis which, at least in the logic of the text (whatever may have been the case in Barth's biography, in Barth's research procedure in constructing a dogmatic locus), plays the role of warrant for an established point of view. Just how prominent this role is can be gathered from the several different introductory clauses that recur constantly in the first phrases of an exegetical excursus. Such, for example, are: "In this connection . . . (e.g. I.2, p. 332), "In this context . . . "(I.2, p. 673), "We are reminded of . . . "(I.2, p. 676), "In this sense . . ." (II.1, p. 365). Each introduces the biblical exegesis in such a way as to indicate that the dogmatic exposition has at least some kind of priority over the exegesis. The priority is not really "logical," nor material; it is indeed more a question of strategy, of tactic, of the rhetoric of theological argument than the precise method of theological inquiry. At any rate, with a large degree of consistency the biblical exegesis clearly has a kind of subordinate, supportive role in reference to the dogmatic exposition. For example, in I.2 (p. 277-8), Barth is insisting doctrinally on a firm distinction between discipleship as imitation (which he rejects) and discipleship as conformity to Christ. The biblical exegesis supporting the point is introduced as follows: "For a right understanding at this point, the decisive New Testament concept . . . ". It then proceeds with an analysis of the concept of "following" Christ. The point is not that the introductory phrases are so important in themselves; they rather indicate what is in fact important, that the biblical exegesis is subordinate to the exposition in the strategy of the argument. In the case of the present example, the New Testament passages yielding the concept "following Christ" are used to support a distinction between *comformitas Christi* and *imitatio Christi*. My point is not to question the validity of the usage, but rather to point out that such a usage occurs as an argumentative strategy. Clearly, the New Testament passages, and the concept "following Christ" (if the Bible even has any concepts) might be better used in support of some other distinction, or may have nothing to do with any concept that might interest a 20th century theologian whatsoever.

To recapitulate: we are concerned in this chapter to highlight theological pressures on Barth's biblical exegesis from the dogmatic exposition in the *Church Dogmatics*. We have seized upon Barth's conceptual-analytical approach in exegesis as the most evident manifestation of theological pressure. The Bible can of course be read in many different ways; but Barth the theologian, perhaps *the* master conceptual analyst of Christian religious language in recent times, not surprisingly reads the Bible as a resource for conceptual analysis. This means first of all that in looking for the biblical witness he reads its diverse literature in terms of the concepts that it employs, concepts that at the same time constitute, refine, and criticize contemporary Christian discourse. Secondly, however, these biblical concepts must themselves be analyzed to determine the specific contours of their content and use. The final chapter of this study will contain a full presentation of the kind of analysis Barth undertakes in his exegesis; for the present, we will concern ourselves with certain aspects of this exegetical analysis that provide evidence of theological pressure on the exegesis from the dogmatic. It is common knowledge that Barth employed dialectical patterns of presentation and analysis in his theology. It is not surprising, then, that such patterns have an echo in his exegesis in the form of repeated, almost formulaic, exegetical devices. They are uniformly dualistic. They are applied to every kind of biblical literature, in every conceivable doctrinal context, and used to support every kind of exegetical position. That is, they seem unrelated to the text under discussion (or only externally related). They appear more like theological habits of mind, carried over into biblical exegesis in the form of statements about the content and intention of the biblical witness. For example, there is the formulaic distinction between the "veiled" and the "unveiled" (or the "revealed" and the "hidden"). Something in the biblical text is said by Barth to be alternately, simultaneously, or sequentially disclosed and kept secret. The content can be anything from an act of God to the motivations behind an act of human sin to the language of the divine creation. For example, in speaking about the relation between Jesus' self-designation as Son of Man and his status as Messiah, Barth states: "Without being able to adduce proof of this, I would prefer to think of this designation in relation to the name Messiah as that of a pseudonym to the correct name, at least as an element of veiling and not of unveiling" (I.2, p. 23). A second example is the formula of "subject" and "predicate," in which some element of the text is said by Barth to be more properly thought of as a logical-grammatical subject, another as predicate. In its own way, of course, I do not deny that such a device can be a highly illuminating exegetical move; I merely wish to point out that it derives from Barth's theological interests, and often serves to render a text useful to his particular theological concern of the

moment.   A typical example is Barth's assertion that
statements in *Romans* about the love of God the
Creator for His creation stand as predicates to the
subject Jesus Christ (I.2, p. 379).   A final example
of   a   formulaic exegetical device for conceptual
analysis is the distinction between an analytic and
synthetic judgement.   Barth's usage roughly corresponds
to the famous definition and status given to this
distinction in the preface to Kant's *Critique of Pure
Reason*, but Barth was no doubt aware of the history of
the distinction in Protestant orthodoxy.   At any rate,
Barth usually means by an analytic judgement a biblical
statement in which a biblical concept is clarified but not
expanded informatively by the addition of further
concepts; a synthetic judgement *is* such an expansive,
informative statement.   Again, Barth uses the device
when expounding narrative, poetry, paranesis, and so
forth; it is a technique for conceptual analysis, not a
designation of the literary form of the text under
discussion.   For example, in discussing the divine
simplicity, in which who God is   and   what   God does
toward us are one simple reality, Barth states in support
of this view: "It is, then, what may be called an analytical
judgement when in Deut. 7.9 God is called the "faithful
God", or in the Song of Moses in Deut. 32.4 the "God of
truth" (II.1, p. 459).
Another evidence of theological pressure on Barth's
exegetical analysis of biblical concepts is what might be
called the high level of doctrinal precision.   Given the
close relation of most of Barth's biblical exegesis to the
immediate doctrinal context in which it occurs, there are
occasions on which a piece of exegesis is rather
unconvincingly introduced as support for a highly
detailed, highly technical moment in Christian
theological discourse.   This is not mandated by Barth's
overall theological method; he rejects the kind of
biblicism that insists that Christian discourse must, at

every turn, item for item, find support in a biblical text.
Nevertheless, such moments are certainly present in
Barth's exegesis, and appear in the form of inappropriate
or anachronistic ascription of doctrinal precision to the
content of the biblical witness. For example, in speaking
of a series of biblical passages from both testaments
employing the concept "glory," Barth writes:

> We cannot fail to see that according to the
> testimony of the Bible the conception of the
> glory of God belongs to the context of the
> doctrine of the love of God. It is a matter of the
> free love of God. This is what we have to bear in
> mind in view of the great objectivity of the
> concept. But it is a matter of God's love. We
> shall not fail to notice this if we do not lose
> sight of the clear soteriological relationship of
> the concept in both Old and New Testaments, its
> relationship to Israel and the Church, its
> concentration in the person of Jesus Christ.
> (II.1, p. 643)

Now, I do not deny that the Bible can be used to support
the several theological positions in this quotation (e.g.
the connection of the doctrine of divine glory to the
doctrine of divine love, its Christocentric, soteriological
interest . . . etc.). I want to point out, however, that this
is meant as *biblical exegesis strictly considered*, not
theology, and as such surely finds in the Bible a level of
doctrinal precision comfortably similar to the
theological concerns it is used to support. In this sense,
the theological concern is exercising an evident
pressure on the exegetical analysis.
      What I have said so far about Barth's conceptual-
analytical approach in exegesis assumes that the usual
function of an exegetical excursus is conceptual support
for a particular theological concept or argument. While
such indeed is the case, it is not entirely uniform; and
significant departures from this usual pattern are worth

noting in this chapter on theological pressures on Barth's biblical exegesis.   The departures involve a different *function* of the biblical exegesis in the overall shape of Barth's theological argument; and the difference in function, in turn, can significantly alter the balance between exegesis and dogmatic exposition. There are some occasions when Barth will actually move the biblical exegesis into the large print.   That is, he is no longer using the Bible in the large print, no longer commenting on it, meditating on it, no longer saying today what one must say on the *basis* of the biblical text; he is, rather, actually expounding the Bible *in place of* such dogmatic reflection.   The effect is, of course,   a   heightened   sense of the importance of the Bible in Barth's theology, as if to illustrate graphically the *immediate availability* of the biblical world.   A good example of this sort is Barth's exposition in the large print of the expectation of Christ in the Old Testament (I.2, pp. 80-101).

Another departure concerns the relative amount of dogmatic exposition and biblical exegesis in a given section of text.   A precise fraction would be hard to determine; but the usual pattern is a majority of actual space and conceptual weight falling to the dogmatic exposition, but with a very strong, though supportive role going to the exegesis.   Barth can depart from this balance in both directions; he can, first of all, construct a section with much less, or indeed little if any, biblical exegesis.   An extreme in this direction would be the one section (actually an entire paragraph, though a short one--for Barth) in these volumes with no biblical exegesis whatsoever: his treatment of the command of God as the judgement of God in para. 39 (II.2, pp. 733-81). In the other direction, Barth can also construct a section which is imbalanced in favor of the biblical exegesis.   I know of no section in the *Church Dogmatics* which is entirely biblical exegesis;   nevertheless,   one section from our volumes will illustrate the extreme in this direction. The section, on the determination of the rejected, is 57 pages long in English, of which 48 pages are detailed biblical exegesis. The dogmatic exposition in this section is, thus, more nearly a theological statement in thesis form that introduces the biblical exegesis to follow. A final departure from the usual function of an exegetical excursus occurs when the exegesis is related to broader divisions of the *Church Dogmatics* than the individual concept. The usual function of an excursus is as a support for the analysis of a single theological concept. There are some few occasions, however, when the biblical exegesis functions to introduce and guide the dogmatic presentation in an* entire sub-section, section, or even paragraph (though never a *locus*). Such cases are Barth's version of the traditional *"locus classicus,"* individual biblical texts with broad assimilative power in organizing and presenting biblical and theological truth. An example of this sort is Barth's citation of John 1.14 ("The Word became flesh") as the leading theme for an entire section on Christology (I.2, pp. 159-71), which then becomes the comprehensive theme for the entire section. Another example, a small exegetical excursus on the command to "honor thy father and mother" in Ex. 20.12, opens and guides a section on authority under the Word of God (I.2, pp. 585-660). Barth begins his exegesis (and the section as a whole, which thus opens with small print): "All that we have still to say about the authority of the Church itself can be understood in the light of the commandment . . . " In such examples, it is as if certain biblical passages have the sort of constructive and assimilative ability that is usually associated with the theological thesis, and Barth is content thus simply to replace the one by the other.

Thus far we have considered, under the rubric of "theological pressures" on Barth's biblical exegesis, the pressure and presence of his own dogmatic exposition and concerns. There is likewise, however, a pressure exerted on the exegesis, not so much from the dogmatic exposition *per se* as from Barth's seemingly unquestioned assumption of the mutual fit of biblical language and traditional Christian theological language. In a sense, this is the single most pervasive characteristic of Barth's biblical exegesis; and its very pervasiveness makes it hard to identify, hard to notice. The mutual fit, the mutual addressability of biblical language and traditional theological language is the condition for the possibility of the kind of biblical exegesis Barth does. As such, it is the very atmosphere in which the exegesis flourishes, rather than being one characteristic among others.

Nevertheless, the pressure exerted by the presence of traditional theological language in Barth's biblical exegesis will from time to time be more palpable; I am referring to the many passages where traditional theological debate, accompanied by the citation of authors, will take place in the biblical exegesis. A good example, in which the reference to tradition is positive, occurs in an exegetical excursus on the Incarnational theology of the New Testament (I.2, pp. 147-9). The excursus runs from a citation and exegesis of several New Testament passages, to consideration of this theological topic in the Fathers (Ignatius, Hippolytus, Athanasius, Augustine, Basilius) to Medieval (Anselm), Reformation (Luther), and Post-Reformation (Polanus) theologies. Barth assumes throughout the excursus a continuity of theme among these several authors; the result is, of course, that coming to terms with the contribution of, say, Anselm, is *ipso facto* a step toward coming to terms with the biblical witness. Barth will just as often press his assumption of the mutual fit of biblical and traditional theological language in a negative direction.   That is, he will use the Bible to criticize a theological author; and he will do so in such a way as to make clear that the condition for the possibility of such a negative reference is the mutual fit of the theological concerns of the Bible and the disputed authority, even though the fit is in this case a negative one. An example of this sort is a passage in II.1 (pp. 279-80) on the nature of God's love. After quoting a number of biblical passages, Barth concludes: "In this light it is difficult or impossible to agree with the doctrine of the love of God as developed by A. Ritschl." That the Bible can, in Barth's hands, be more or less immediately used to discriminate against certain traditional theological options says a great deal about Barth's handling of the Bible (as well as, of course, his view of his opponents).

Another evidence of the pressure of traditional theological language on Barth's biblical exegesis is Barth's frequent attempt to square his own biblical exegesis with classical Christian biblical exegesis. The most common form this takes is a reference to the exegesis of Luther and Calvin, though other authors are often used. A good example is an excursus in I.1 (pp. 457-9) in which Barth begins with two or so pages of his own biblical exegesis (on the concept of divine sonship) and then follows with a page of quotations from Luther's exegesis. Or, a similar example in I.2 (pp. 120-1) on the function of John the Baptist in the New Testament follows the form: Barth's exegesis, citation of Calvin, citation of Luther. The point is not just that Barth was guided in his exegesis of the Bible by his reading of classical Christian biblical exegesis, though this too is an interesting and noteworthy fact. But the point is also that Barth did so *in principle*, that is, that he considered the mutual fit of his own biblical exegesis and classical

Christian exegesis a basic requirement. Just how principled the reference to Luther and Calvin is can be seen most clearly in those passages in which their exegesis becomes, not just a revered and necessary secondary authority, but *the text itself*. As one example of a dozen or so instances from these volumes, consider the following introduction to an exegetical-theological excursus on the doctrine of the Holy Spirit: "For the biblical background and the historical context of this exposition, the wealth of adducible material is so great that we must confine ourselves to only one classical document, the foundation which Calvin prefixed to his great exposition of *modus percipiendae Christi gratiae* (Inst. III.1)" (I.2, p. 240). It is important that such a heading introduces a basically *exegetical*, not a basically *historical*, excursus.

Much like the basic confidence that Barth exercises in the mutual fit of biblical and traditional theological language, he exercises as well a confidence that diverse biblical texts mutually address one another. He exercises, that is, a confidence that one can move from passage to passage, from book to book, from canonical section to canonical section, in a *disciplined* way ("scientific" or "technical"); in a way therefore that is open to meaningful criticism, dispute, and correction, and in a way that is fundamentally an *advance* on the exegesis of a single text in isolation. Thus, other biblical passages (or Barth's understanding of them) exercise an enormous pressure on the exegesis of any given biblical text. Like traditional theological language, the pressure and presence of other biblical passages is a condition for the possibility of the kind of exegesis Barth does, and is therefore pervasive throughout the *Church Dogmatics*.

Evidence for the pressure exercised by other biblical texts are the so-called parallel passages, which are mutually addressable biblical texts. These are of two very different sorts. The first are cumulative and complementary. Two or more passages are juxtaposed in such a way that together they yield a biblical concept as a whole that is greater than the sum of the individual parts. This type of parallel textual exegesis is the backbone of Barth's exegetical corpus, and it exudes an almost audacious, though in its own way carefully controlled, confidence in the ultimate unity of the biblical witness. A good example is an excursus on freedom (I.2, pp. 260-5) which *exegetes* (not just cites, or quotes) passages from Matthew, John, Mark, Luke, Romans, I John, Ephesians, Colossians, 2 Corinthians, 2 Timothy, Galatians, Isaiah, and the Psalter (and it closes with passages from Calvin and Luther!) The range is audacious, and to some schools of thought patently undisciplined (certainly unhistorical). Nevertheless, in Barth's hands the movement from passage to passage, the cumulative, controlled weaving of a piece of exegetical fabric, is surely anything but imprecise, or tendentious, or "ideological" as opposed to "historical." Historical criticism it is not; nor, however, is it anything but expertly crafted and technically sophisticated to a reader not tied to one small conception of the nature of the historical question.

A second type of parallel passage is the *corrective*, which in turn can be either supportive or critical. The supportive passage has the function of clarifying the ambiguous, and is Barth's version of the ancient practice of reading the less clear in light of the more clear. Consider, for example, an excursus on love for God in which Barth raises the exegetical question whether such love can finally be lost for the believer (I.2, pp. 398-400). The framework of the excursus (leaving out some detail) is as follows. He first cites Mt. 24.12 and Rev. 2.4, and asks whether or not these passages might be said to refer to a love for God that has been lost due to persecution. Considered in themselves, they are ambiguous. He then cites passages from Rom., I Cor. 13, and I Jn., which unambiguously refer to the permanence of love for God among true believers, despite, or even because of, adverse circumstances. He concludes, therefore, that "it is impossible" for the disputed reading to contradict directly the sure testimony of these others, and glosses them with the interpretation that corresponds accordingly. An example of a critical corrective passage can be found in II.1 (pp. 103-5) in a section on the question of natural theology. After citing several passages from the Psalms seeming to support the notion of revelation in nature, Barth cites passages from the Psalms testifying to the universality of human sin, and the universal need for divine grace in the knowledge of God. He concludes: "Do these passages not decide at once the way in which certain other passages in the Psalms most definitely cannot be understood?" (p. 204). Instances of this latter sort of parallel passage are indeed the most extreme form of the pressure exercized by one biblical text upon the exegesis of another, so much so that one might better speak of supplanting rather than critically correcting.

Example C: Following Christ

We are considering in this chapter pressures from Barth's theological scholarship and concerns on Barth's biblical exegesis. As the third in our series of exegetical excursuses for close analysis, attention will be given to an excursus from II.2 on the determination of the elect. The text has been chosen because it evinces a representative amount, type, and style of such theological pressures.

The text occurs in paragraph 35 on the election of the individual. Barth considers first, in this paragraph, the person of Jesus Christ in election, then the distinction between election and rejection, and finally the "determination" of the elect individual--the section in which our text occurs. The exegetical excursus itself constitutes over half the section. The dogmatic exposition in the main body of the text precedes the exegesis (the usual order), and presents in rather summary, almost colloquial language the main concepts of the section. In this case, as in many others in the *Church Dogmatics*, there is a rough isomorphism between the concepts in the dogmatic exposition and the biblical exegesis.

The question which Barth is addressing in this section is as follows. Granted that all Christian election is election in Jesus Christ, and thus entirely sovereign and gracious on God's part; and granted that God's electing grace is far superior over, and even envelops within itself, God's rejecting choice; just what is the *aim* of the election of the individual? What is he or she elected for? Where are they to go? What are they to do? For what *purpose* are they elect? Barth calls these questions the problem of the *life-content* of the elect individual. What is this life-content to be?--such is the topic of this section, and the general topic for the exegetical excursus under study.

Now, the excursus is composed of an attempt to answer this question of the life-content of the elect individual in the form of an analytical presentation of a series of biblical-theological "concepts." As will be recalled, our contention in this chapter has been that a major sign of the presence of Barth's theological concerns in his biblical exegesis is the very conceptual-analytical method that he so often employs in the exegesis. We shall thus be concerned to show in this section how it is that the form and content of the biblical exegesis in this excursus shows evidence of Barth's broader theological concerns. We shall proceed by examining each of the major concepts in turn. Barth begins the excursus with an introductory section. While not of immediate interest to the topic of our chapter, it is important for the excursus as a whole, and illustrates problems we have discussed already in chapter two of this study. The introduction states why it is that Barth can find a life-content for the elect individual *only* in the New Testament. The Old Testament, according to Barth, lacks such a profile because it lacks the full reality of Jesus Christ. Without this reality, the various threads of the Old Testament picture of God, and its picture of the elect individual, lead off into several disunited directions. Consequently, an exegetical analysis of this topic can use only New Testament passages--as is in fact the case with our excursus. It is interesting to note, though only as an aside in the present context, that our exegetical excursus is one of the very few in which Barth holds that the Old Testament, whether heavily Christianized or not, simply offers no answer to the question under discussion.

What is the life-content of the elect individual? The first answer of Barth's exegesis of the New Testament is the concept of "witness." The individual believer is elected to bear witness to Christ. Barth offers this concept after a brief mention of the problem of the *scope* of the election, the question of universal or limited election and salvation, and clearly frames his answer to the problem of the life-content of the elect individual in terms of the question of those who have not heard the gospel and thus faced the question of their election. In other words, the exegetical-theological concept of witness already has a certain contour because of the *function* it performs in answering a need. According to Barth, the New Testament concept of witness is to be directed *against* the classical Christian doctrine of predestination, with its orientation towards the private, personal concern of eternal salvation and blessedness. Though opposites in this case, the New Testament and classical Christian language are certainly commensurable in Barth's eyes, and no space whatsoever is given over to the hermeneutical task of the fusion of horizons. Biblical language about election and classical Christian language about election have a kind of direct co-presence to one another; no walls need breaking down to hear the biblical voice because none have been erected. It is interesting to note that Barth ascribes the error of classical Christian doctrine on this score to the lack of attention to the Christological focus of the problem. If the person of Jesus Christ had been consistently kept in mind the doctrine would not have gone astray. So Barth says; however, beyond a few vague references to the function of Jesus Christ in the New Testament of bearing witness to Himself (no passages are cited), the "person of Jesus Christ" plays little or no part in Barth's conceptual analysis of election to witness. This is a common problem in reading some of Barth's exegesis; he often loudly affirms his own Christocentricity, and then proceeds with little or no trace of it.

The individual believer is elected to bear witness; armed with this concept, Barth tackles the exegetical problem, in two parts. He first asks concerning the precise function of bearing witness in the New Testament. He offers in answer an exposition of several passages from Revelation involving the heavenly choir singing glory to God in eternity. Chief among these passages is that concerning the twenty-four elders (Rev. 4.10) who fall down before Him who sits on the throne and sing His praises. Barth's exegetical point is that the company *falls* before Him and *sings*; that is, that they *actively* engage in their blessedness, rather than *passively* enjoying it. And what they do is to use their voice, to utter a word to and about the one whom they adore.   And so, the profile of the elect is an active participation in their calling by attesting the one who calls; such, in fact, is the concept of witness.   Now, two things need pointing out about Barth's analysis.   Firstly, whether he is right or wrong in his exegesis, the conceptual problem which he brings to the text goes a long way   toward   contributing   to   the   answer.   The question that he brings to the text is certainly not the only one that might be brought; and other questions, other *theological* questions, would yield a very different exegesis.   Secondly, Barth employs here a move that is familiar to readers of the *Church Dogmatics* as a whole.   Though Barth often seems to see Christian discourse as a storied universe with distinct moments in time, he often merges these moments, in doctrine and in exegesis, into what approximates a unified, non-temporal view (cf. the doctrine of the Trinity in I.1).   In this instance, though he acknowledges that the biblical depiction concerns a real *future* for the church and the world, he reads this future back into the present to answer the question concerning the temporal life-content of the elect, and concludes that "both in this world as in the coming one, according to the New Testament, the elect are not merely saved and blessed, but as such they are the bearers of that mighty voice from   heaven" (p.   424).[2]   The point is that in this instance at least a biblical concept seems to sublimate the narrative shape of the biblical witness.

Barth then turns to the *content* of the witness which the elect are to bear.   Not surprisingly, that content is the *person* of Jesus Christ, an idea met often enough in this   study   that it need not be repeated here.   It is

[2] The English edition of the *Church   Dogmatics* has mistakenly deleted the phrase "as in the coming one" (*wie in der kuenftigen--K.D.*, II.2, p. 469).

interesting to note that in raising directly the Christological focus of the concept of Christian witness Barth has seemingly turned his attention toward the concept of witness as such, as opposed to the concept as an answer to the question of the life-content of the elect. Almost as an extended aside, as an attempt to round off the analysis of the concept, Barth digresses from the function which the concept performs in this excursus to the general content of the concept in biblical-theological discourse. This textual strategy accounts in part for the extraordinarily repetitious quality of much of Barth's exegesis, as well as for the inordinate length. An any rate, Barth completes his exegetical analysis of the concept of witness by another reference to the centrality of Jesus Christ.

The second concept with which Barth answers the question concerning the life-content of the elect individual in the Bible is the concept of *community*: the elect individual is elected to participation in the community of faith, or the church, which Barth defines in good Reformation fashion as the fellowship of those who have in faith responded to the call of Jesus Christ by the power of the Holy Spirit (pp. 426-30). This section is a good example of Barth's technique of exegetical concept-building. It must not be supposed that an exegetical concept necessarily corresponds to what might be called a biblical "theme," a positive moment in the biblical message. A concept can, as in this instance, be built from material that is more or less around the edges of the biblical text. Barth finds the passages in the New Testament which attest God's election, and notices the close proximity of passages attesting the Christian community. Thus, a concept is born: election is election to community. No positive texts--texts, that is, which make it there special point to make and elaborate upon this equation--are necessary. The presence of the equation in the text is further highlighted by the fact that Barth allows an inference to build the concept. Belief in Jesus Christ is always ecclesial belief; therefore, election to belief is always election to the church. At a stroke a further series of passages around the edges of the Bible are added to the formation of the concept.

It is important to keep in mind at this point that we are dealing with Barth's biblical exegesis, not his theological exposition. The concept which he builds is an exegetical concept, not first of all a theological one. The concept is meant therefore to organize and articulate the biblical witness to the issue under discussion. Now, I do not wish to dispute whether or not Barth has adequately rendered the biblical texts in his presentation and analysis of the concept of community. It should be said, however, that Barth has here judged a timeless theological problem with an exegetical argument. According to Barth, the Bible unambiguously supports the equation election--community--individual rather than election--individual--community. Whole sections of Christendom are thus dealt a blow by Barth through biblical exegesis, not theological argument. The point is: whether he is right or wrong in his analysis, the fact that *so much* can ride on an exegetical concept that is in turn built on material around the edges of the biblical witness seems an odd, and noteworthy, procedure. Theological dispute is unnecessary precisely where it would seem most welcome; it is unnecessary because, according to Barth, there never should have been a question about the Bible's teaching in the first place.

Why does Barth entertain what might be considered a misplaced conception of the Bible's precision about the equation of election and community? A phrase from the excursus might provide the clue: "All the predicates of the elect individual are predicates which apply originally to Jesus Christ, and then, in and by Him, to His own, who believe in Him, but to all believers in the same way, with no basic difference" (p. 427). This is offered as a gloss on New Testament passages of election. Now, it does not seem inappropriate or inaccurate to argue that the real concern of this sentence, and the real concern of Barth's concept of community, is the preservation of the centrality of the subject *Jesus Christ*. Using the formal device of predicates and subject which we have remarked on earlier in the chapter, Barth is trying to insure that *Jesus Christ* alone is the true possessor of the predicates of election, and that this one true Subject is not lost in the sea of a plurality of subjects. The logical priority of the community over the individual guarantees the epiphenomenal character of plural subjects, as well as the condition for the possibility of having one true Subject of all predicates of election. Again, I do not dispute whether Barth was right or wrong in his theological concern; I wish to point out what is rather hidden in the excursus as it is offered, namely the large presence of a theological concern in an exegetical section. If indeed this material evinces a misplaced conception of the Bible's precision on this topic, it means that theological discussion has been prematurely truncated by the loss of exegetical richness and variety.

We move now, following Barth, to the concept of *apostleship* (pp. 430-49), though of course in doing so we are not really moving away from *witness* and *community*; exegetical concepts, like theological ones, are analyzed cumulatively, so that previous conceptual points made are allowed to flow right into the current stage of the discussion. The concept of apostleship, in answer to the question of the life-content of the elect individual, is actually a master-concept having three aspects: the call, the appointment, and the commission. The three aspects are mapped onto a sequence in the synoptic gospels, the nodal-points of which are determined by the shape of Christ's story (Galilean ministry, rode to Jerusalem, resurrection and ascension). We shall shortly turn to each of these aspects in turn, but it is instructive to notice certain features of the master-concept of apostleship. Firstly, the three aspects are related to Christology not just narrative-sequentially, but also conceptually; Barth specifically mentions Christ's threefold office (prophet, priest, and king) in such a way as to make clear that it is the master pattern of which apostleship is a copy. Thus, the exegetical answer to the question of the life-content of the elect individual once again reaffirms Barth's tendency to argue that there is really only one Life-Content. Indeed, this tendency is likewise promoted by his general conception of apostleship. Like Christ Himself, the twelve apostles (the definite number is important to Barth as a symbol) are not just *the* historical origin for the church, they in some sense *are* the church. The relation between the apostles and the church, then and now, is *conceptual*, not merely *historical*. The twelve apostles act as a kind of buffer between Christ and the company of Christians, so that the "predicates" of Christ, in being communicated to those who are not Christ, do not get lost in a sea of plural subjects. Finally Barth treats of the sub-concepts in reverse order to their narrative sequence. The framework of the material is narrative, and Barth honors that in the analysis he provides; but it *is* conceptual analysis, not or not only narrative retelling, and the conceptual analysis can be sharpened by reversing the narrative sequence. Here is no biography of the apostles.

The first concept (under the general concept of apostleship) is the concept of the apostolic *commission* (pp. 432-5), which is given the smallest space by Barth, but the greatest weight. It is based on Mt. 28, Lk. 24, and Acts 1, each of which is given a straightforward summary of its contents by Barth. Barth further acknowledges the great differences between the Matthean and the Lukan version of the final commission. He nevertheless argues that they have a common content, a common witness; and this move is in turn based on the conceptual-analytical method that Barth brings to the text. Faced with a question like that of the life-content of the individual elect, and armed with a concept like that of apostleship, sequential variety or contradiction in bibilical texts is rarely problematic, and often contributes to the final exegesis that Barth provides. Conceptual analysis does not ignore narrative sequence, it interprets it; conceptual analysis does not therefore ignore sequential variety or contradiction, but interprets it. As Barth says: "The actual teaching given us by these variants is obviously more important than the historical difficulty which we may legitimately feel . . . " They have a "common content", which Barth states as follows: "The person of Jesus Himself was still necessary to create for them the relationship to Him which enabled them, as sent by Him, to perform what He performed" (p. 433). Such is the first aspect of apostleship, though the last moment in the sequence of its unfolding: Christ is the commission which He Himself gives to these others.

The second concept under the master-concept of apostleship is that of apostolic *appointment*, which has its narrative setting according to Barth in the middle period of Jesus' story, the road from Galilee to Jerusalem (pp. 435-42). In this passage of the excursus, Barth employs a frequently used exegetical technique for forming his concept of appointment. No fewer than 40 biblical texts are quoted in these pages, with Barth's exegetical contribution being little more than providing a minimal amount of discourse structure. The technique, that is, is to avoid the close analysis of biblical texts (though there is some of that too, as we shall see), and to instead allow the rapid-fire quotation of scores of biblical texts to form an impression of the idea. The yield is not precise knowledge or analysis of any one of the biblical texts, but usually a summary content of the "biblical concept"--in this case the concept of apostolic appointment in the second period of Jesus' story. The key to the success of this technique is Barth's ability to convince the reader that the texts have in common a shared "concept" that can be analyzed out of them. Barth's method for inspiring such confidence is to assume that no other reading is really even possible; the texts are there simply to yield such a concept. A common stylistic device used in such contexts is to begin several sentences with 'obviously," "clearly," or "it is impossible not to see that . . . "

The outcome of these multiple biblical references is a concept of the apostles during this period of Jesus' activity. According to Barth, the picture is "one of absolute blindness in face of the way which Jesus has chosen for Himself, and in face of the fact that He will and must follow it to the end. Again, it is one of absolute misunderstanding about the manner in which they may follow and serve Him. Again, it is one of absolute error about their own capacity to follow Him. Again, it is one of absolutely wrong ideas about that which they may anticipate for themselves in following Him. Finally, it is one of absolute denial in practice at the moment when they ought to make good their insights and resolve, and actually follow Him" (p. 439). Absolute blindness, absolute misunderstanding, absolute error, absolutely wrong ideas, absolute denial; such is the picture of apostleship. And obviously, the main point is the customary reference of Barth, already said by Him to be the main point of the third stage of apostolic commission (treated above) as well: "The positive aspect of the picture seen in this second, middle stage of their calling and appointment is that He is for them, watching for them, praying, humbling Himself, serving, accepting the cross in His death and passion" (p. 439). Now, two points are in order concerning Barth's conceptual analysis. Firstly, it is surely a sign of a *restrictive* presence of the theological concerns in the biblical exegesis when scores of gospel pericopes are said to yield such an unnuanced "concept." This is not to deny that the concept is "biblical"; it is rather to make the more formal point that this particular method of finding a biblical concept--the method of dozens of quotations interlaced with comments--is sure to fail at times to inspire confidence that the concept arises from the material. Secondly, however, it is worth noting that the exegetical concepts seem inappropriate to the *theological* concerns. Recall that the question concerns the life-content of the individual elect person. Barth has decided to answer the question by an analysis of New Testament apostleship; and the yield of his analysis of the middle section of the gospels is a kind of *non*life-content of the elect. Of all the pericopes on discipleship in these texts, Barth draws out a picture which is entirely unusable in answering the question that he has posed (except to deny that the question has any meaning in Christian discourse). The point is that, while the conceptual analysis of biblical texts can seem to take on a life of its own independent of the biblical texts, it can also do so independent of the *theological problem*. That is, a biblical-theological concept in an excursus can seem to hover somewhere between the Bible and the Dogmatics, touching both, and yet at times moving off in an entirely different direction.

As mentioned above, Barth does give one piece of extended exegesis in this section: an exegesis of the confession of Peter in Mt. 16. Only two salient features of his exegesis will here be pointed out, as evidence of the presence of theological pressure on the exegesis. Firstly, Barth considers Peter's confession a "hidden" confession, only to be revealed at the resurrection of Jesus from the dead.   That is, the confession of Peter is an *anticipation*, a proleptic reference to the presence of the resurrected Christ.   This reading conforms to the biblical-theological view that Barth held at this time that all faith of the disciples in Jesus arises solely from the resurrection; all references to faith in the gospels before   the   resurrection   must be referred forward to it as their hidden source, regardless of the immediate context of the response.   (Later in the *Church Dogmatics* Barth changed his mind, and began to make theological mileage out of the faith occurrences in the gospels before the resurrection in their immediate contexts in Jesus' story).   Secondly, it is the *sinful* Peter of whom Jesus says that upon him will be built the church.   That is, it is precisely the absolute failure as an apostle that Barth has drawn out of this period in the gospels which receives the blessing, not, or not only, the Peter of the "hidden" confession of faith in Christ's Messiahship.   How does Barth know that such is the purpose of Jesus' words?   Says Barth: "Self-evidently it is not the special integrity or loyalty to principle of the man Peter and his companions which constitutes the foundation and invincibility of the Church.   We know what they were like" (p. 441).   It is the picture of apostleship that Barth has painted conceptually that is used to provide the context for Christ's statement, not the confession of Peter.   Given Barth's view of apostleship during this period it couldn't be any other way.

We turn, now, to the final concept in this exegetical excursus: the concept of the *calling* of the apostles (pp. 442-9).   Already at the beginning of the analysis one meets with a familiar formal move by Barth: the call of the apostles, corresponding to the first, or Galilean stage of Jesus' story, is simply a *veiled* reference forward to   the   second   and especially   the   third stage of the sequence of apostolic development.   Thus, the dualism veiled-unveiled is used here,   as it so often is, to give a variety of texts one comprehensive meaning (often enough collapsing the narrative sequence).   In this instance all the hundreds of pericopes involving the apostles in the gospels have been declared ultimately a concealed reference to the Great Commission.   And, of course, because of the nature of the Great Commission-- the   apostles   are   to   bear   witness   to   Christ--the exegetical move serves to reinforce Barth's conviction that Jesus Christ is really the only true apostle.   At any rate, Barth's comprehensive view of the apostolic call in the first section of the gospels is that they are called, having no regard to their previous situation, to bear witness to Christ.   It is of course a conceptual connection rather than an exegetical one, but when Barth goes on to assert that Jesus' election of the apostles is isomorphic with his election of individual believers, an answer to the question of the life-content of the elect individual is born--they are elected, called, to bear witness.   The effect of this conceptual connection is to make a biblical text immediately accessible to an arresting conceptual problem for any reader of the Bible (how am I to see myself in relationship to Jesus Christ?), as well as to provide an exegetical basis for Barth's answer.

Among the texts with which Barth deals one series in particular will be considered here.   Barth expounds the synoptic gospels' account of the. actual appointment of the twelve.   More precisely, Barth expounds the preface, the   immediately   preceding   context,   for   this appointment.   Recall that in Mark, Jesus goes up on the mountain (3.13), which is expanded by Luke to include a night of prayer (Lk. 6.12).   In Matthew, the text which immediately precedes Jesus' appointment of the twelve in 10.1 is a general statement about Jesus going about the cities and villages preaching and healing; the text continues that Christ had compassion on the crowds, and invited the disciples to pray with him to God to send out workers into the harvest (Mt. 9.35-8). Now, clearly enough the Matthean account on the one side, and the Markan and Lukan account on the other, seem to point in very different directions. Not surprisingly, Barth considers the narrative contradiction "significant and instructive," and turns to pursue its interpretation. Notice, however, what he does *not* do to interpret these texts. He of course does not pursue an historical referent which would be such as to give rise to these two different accounts; he in fact does not look behind the texts at all, historically. Nor, however, does he interpret the differences in terms of the tendencies of the individual gospels. He does of course concern himself with what Mark is trying to say, and Luke, and Matthew, but not in order better to understand the individual gospels. What he *does* do, is to ask of these texts what they are trying to say in *common* (even if in narrative contradiction) about the appointment of the apostles. Says Barth: "The question which account is correct is again a pointless one. We would actually have to complete and explain the one by the other even if we had only the one or the other and therefore an unambiguous report" (p. 445). Mark-Luke have Jesus in solitude before God; Matthew has Jesus in compassionate solitude before the multitude; the common content, the conceptual unity which these texts provide concerning the apostolic call, is that the apostles must follow Christ into this solitude before God and before others; being with this Christ is the essence of apostleship. The point I wish to make for the purposes of this chapter, and the point with which we will close this chapter, is that a conceptual-analytical approach has solved an otherwise troublesome exegetical problem. Armed with the concept of the apostolic call, Barth is able to interpret *conceptually* a narrative contradiction. The overriding theological concern--the analysis of the concept of the apostolic call in partial answer   to the question   of   the life-content of the elect individual--is the condition for the possibility of the kind of exegesis Barth provides.

CHAPTER 4

Explication of the Text

Thus far in our study we have concentrated on major aspects of Barth's biblical exegesis. Our attention has thus far been focused on the exegesis itself in an attempt to identify and analyze the main characteristics of the hundreds of exegetical excursuses that occur in the volumes of the *Church Dogmatics* under study. Three aspects in particular have held our attention in the three previous chapters: the search for the Bible's *witness*, the *Christocentricity* of exegesis, and the various aspects of Bath's *theological presence* in the biblical exegesis.

In this final chapter we shall continue to be concerned with the biblical exegesis; however, the focus of our attention will be slightly shifted. We ask in this final chapter concerning the relation of Barth's exegesis to the biblical text itself. We shift our focus, that is, away from the biblical exegesis considered in itself, and toward the biblical exegesis as a response to the text of Holy Scripture. Thus, our question for the final chapter is simply this: here on the one hand is the text, or texts, of Holy Scripture, and here on the other hand is Barth's exegesis; now, how does one move from the one to the other? There is a text, here is exegesis; in what consists this movement from there to here? The concept which has been used in this chapter to answer this question is *explication*; the task of exegesis is the explication of the biblical text. In part, the word explication has been chosen because of the emphasis that Barth places, and that has been placed in this chapter, on the biblical text itself. The text itself is the beginning, middle, and end of exegesis; other factors may enter in, but at no time in Barth's exegesis (or hermeneutic) are they given independent interest or status. Barth, for example, had no interest in reader-response criticism or its contemporary equivalents. According to Barth it was the orthodox Protestant collapsing of the Spirit into the text of the Bible that gave birth to the modern idea of the "reader." The individual, in reading the Bible, came to have immediate access to the Spirit of God in the Bible; the "reader" was born, as was, consequently, attention to his or her status, role, condition, and response. Now, Barth did not so much deny the role of the reader, as to dissolve this historical movement that gave rise to it in the first place. A renewed understanding of the *proclaimed* word of God as the true response to Holy Scripture in the Spirit of God circumscribes and delimits the role of the reader in favor of the content of the text as such. Or again, Barth's scorn for the historical-critical concept of truth-as-historical-reference is due to the concentration of his theological interest in the text itself (rather than as the source for knowledge of something else) and not to any independent doubts concerning the internal integrity of the historical-critical method.

Exegesis is concerned with the biblical text as such. It is concerned to interpret the text by explicating it; that is, it is concerned to expound the text as an end in itself, and not as the means to something else. Barth is thus squarely within the tradition of the *sensus literalis* in that explication of the sense of the text is not considered the foundation for something else (e.g. the multiple senses), but as the goal of all exegesis. This conception of Barth's is aided by the fact that he seems often to consider the Bible as an independent, acting Subject. It speaks; it wants to say this and not that; it warns us here, comforts us there; it is trying to tell us this, and not that. It is *alive*, and so need not be brought to life. Explication is letter *and* spirit.

We shall be concerned in this final chapter to paint a picture of Barth's explication of the biblical text. There will at times be some mention of earlier material, only now from the point of view of the relation of the biblical exegesis to the biblical text rather than from an interest in certain aspects of the exegesis considered in itself. Two broad devices are used by Barth in explicating the biblical text: conceptual analysis and narrative exegesis. We shall consider each in turn, and then how they relate to one another.

Concept and Narrative

The majority of exegetical excursuses in these volumes of the *Church Dogmatics*, as well as in the remaining volumes, is without doubt of the sort that we will here call *conceptual analysis*. We will have occasion, later in this chapter, to speak of narrative exegesis in the *Church Dogmatics*, and will then be in a position to raise the question of the relation of narrative exegesis and exegesis as conceptual analysis; regardless of what we will have to say on these topics, however, there is no doubt that the preponderance of Barth's exegesis is conceptual analysis.

In order to describe what is meant by exegesis as
conceptual analysis,   it is first necessary to recall what
is, for Barth, the basic purpose of dogmatics, and what is
the material for enacting this purpose.   The
comprehensive aim of the *Church Dogmatics* is, as
stated in the opening thesis of the work, the "scientific
self-examination of the Christian Church with respect to
the content of its distinctive talk about God" (I.1, p. 3).
The 'distinctive talk' to which Barth refers is later in the
volume clarified specifically as church proclamation;
church proclamation is the "stuff" of dogmatics, the
material with which it works, and whose 'scientific
examination' is its aim.   But what does this mean in
practice?   In the final methodological sections of the
Prolegomena, Barth spells this out in detail: "If we ask
concerning the subject-matter of dogmatics, the reply
must be that it consists essentially in the totality of
what it hears from the Church--the contemporary
church--as its human speech about God.   In practice,
however, it will consist in certain key-words and
fundamental outlines which in this heterogeneous mass
constitute that which is common to the whole and recurs
in all its forms."   Barth goes on to provide a basic
summary of these key-words and outlines: "Up to and
including our own time, when the church has spoken
about God with almost unbroken constancy and
completeness, it has spoken in one way or another about
a Lord of the world and of man, and about His action in
connection with the coming of Jesus Christ.   In one way
or another it has described the world as the creation of
this God, and man as His creature called to special
obedience towards Him.   In one way or another it has
spoken of the sin of man and of his reconciliation with
God, of the life of the Church as a whole and in its
members, and finally of a hope of immortality founded in
the knowledge of God and of His action" (I.2, pp. 778-9).
God, creation, man, sin, and so forth; such are the key-

words of proclamation, and as such constitute the conceptual stuff of dogmatics.[1] Now, the task of the church in dogmatics is the critical examination of this confession with reference to the Word of God as it is attested in Holy Scripture. Exegesis examines the biblical basis for this criticism. Biblical exegesis therefore, to be relevant to the task of dogmatics as a whole, must deal with the same 'stuff' as dogmatics--the basic concepts of the church's confession. Because the comprehensive intentionality of the biblical witness is kerygmatic, and because the Bible's kerygma is largely isomorphic with the confession of the church, in reading the Bible with the concepts of the church's confession in mind one is also reading the Bible "biblically" (as Barth would say). Nevertheless, there is absolutely no biblical exegesis in the *Church Dogmatics* that is not adapted to the purpose of the church's theological self examination.

Turn to any page of biblical exegesis in the *Church Dogmatics*, and one will likely (though not always) find Barth analyzing a biblical concept. Turn back a few pages and one will find Barth using the same, or a similar, concept in a technically and rhetorically very different context of analysis and presentation. Then turn back to the exegesis, and one will likely be impressed at how insistent Barth is that the biblical text should have its own voice in the antiphonal conversation taking place. The point of any given example of conceptual analysis in an exegetical excursus is simply to halt before the biblical text, to allow it a voice, to invite and encourage

---

[1] It will not go unnoticed that the content of church proclamation through the ages as summarized by Barth bears a striking resemblance to the apostle's creed, though it is not founded upon it (nor is the *Church Dogmatics* as a whole). It will also not go unnoticed that the fundamental outline in this particular summary of the church's confession is narrative in form; we shall return to this fact later in the chapter.

the reader simply to notice *what is there* in the biblical text.   Much of this analytical procedure is taken up by quotation of one after another of biblical texts accompanied by paraphrastic restatement ' of particular phrases, statements, verses, or pericopes. But the paraphrase is intended to bend the text toward the conceptual issue at hand in the excursus. The ultimate aim is to determine *biblical usage*; to mull over a series of biblical texts, to describe, to analyze, to sift, to clarify, until biblical usage, until the biblical *witness*, emerges clear and definitive.[2]

It is important to make clear the distinction between a biblical concept and biblical usage as it relates to Barth's exegesis. Biblical usage is the language of the biblical text itself, the narrative, paranesis, hymns, prophecy, and so forth that constitute the utterance meaning of biblical language. Early on in his career Barth called this the "new world" of the Bible, the world that is constituted, indeed created, by biblical religious usage. A biblical concept on the other hand, is a tool for a reader to find himself or herself located in this new world. It is an attempt to harness biblical usage for the task of explicating the text in the context of the responsibility of the Christian church. It is an analysis of biblical usage which aims toward a definitive, normative statement of the biblical witness to a particular problem or moment of Christian proclamation. There cannot, then, be something like a final "list" of biblical concepts complete with a catalogue of definitive analyses; and this because there is not a single,   definitive attempt to

---

[2]I see no reason to align Barth's version of "how to do things with words" with any other particular version. He can at times be favorably compared to New Criticism among literary critics, to performative utterance philosophers, or to a cultural anthropologist like Clifford Geertz. But Barth's enterprise is sufficiently field-specific that it would be difficult to specify precisely any shared features beyond family resemblances.

locate oneself, or find oneself located, in the biblical world. The Reformers' exegesis, for example, cannot supplant our own. However, having made this distinction between usage and concept, it is important to point out that the purpose of the distinction has little or nothing to do, in Barth's eyes, with the highlighting or augmentation of the role of the reader in the formation of biblical concepts. Biblical concepts are to be distinguished from biblical usage not in favor of the freedom of the reader to form concepts (though with this responsibility comes this freedom too, and the freedom is not inconsiderable), but in favor of the freedom of the *biblical text*, biblical usage, to correct and judge the conceptual analysis of it. And I make this statement as a gloss on Barth's *exegesis* (though it is also a part of his hermeneutics), in that Barth's conceptual analysis is always written as if it is content to leave the final word to the usage itself.

Barth takes up the task of biblical exegesis in an attempt to criticize and correct the proclamation of the Christian church. Much of this exegesis involves careful mapping of biblical usage in an attempt to apprehend the "biblical concept of x." Often this is clearly done with a concordance at his side (though only a German one for the Old Testament!), in that a particular family of lexical entries will provide the number and organization of biblical passages under consideration. Often, however, the several passages share no lexical overlapping at all; they can then either reflect a traditional *catena* of biblical citations for a particular concept, or they can, more likely, be an entirely new juxtaposition of previously unrelated texts. Whether lexically related, a traditional *catena*, or (most often) Barth's own new tracing of biblical usage, the biblical texts which Barth uses in the formation of a concept are always cited by Barth, always treated by Barth, as if they are *just the right* combination of texts to solve the conceptual problem.   The method for selection seems more arbitrary; the aim of the selection is however anything but arbitrary, and the analysis that is provided exudes the sense that these texts have joined themselves together as voices in a choir needing Barth only to record their particular chorus.   Lifeless grammatical-etymological analysis of biblical words it is not. There remains to be considered one final problem under the heading of conceptual analysis.   Just what is the ontological status of a "concept" in Barth's biblical exegesis?   Is it real or mental?   Is it ideational or behavioral?   Barth nowhere addresses this question independently of his actual exegesis.   He often speaks of the "biblical concept of x" as if it is something that the Bible itself *possesses*, almost like a physical property. Then again, he will also work with a concept as if it is something that we must form in our minds in response to biblical usage.   These, and similar, ambiguities about "concepts" in Barth's exegesis, are significant in that they illustrate just how much what might be called the horizontal dimension of conceptual analysis is overshadowed by the vertical.   What is relatively unimportant is any particular version of the nature of human concepts (the horizontal dimension); what is important, vastly more important than anything else, is whether or not a piece of conceptual analysis has aptly attested the Word of God (the vertical dimension).   The intrinsic, ontological status of concepts is vastly overshadowed by this, their extrinsic, relational status. Barth does not even address the former question, and in his actual exegesis will sometimes look like an Anglo-American linguistic analyst, sometimes like a phenomonologist, sometimes indeed like an unreconstructed medieval realist.   *Methodus est arbitraria.*   What is addressed, what indeed constitutes the question of all biblical exegesis, is whether the conceptual analysis he has provided adequately captures, or is captured by, the biblical witness to the Word of God; it is this relation to the Word of God which constitutes a concept, whether to its shame or to its glory. *Non sermoni res sed rei sermo subjectus est.* We have now completed our presentation of Barth the conceptual analyst of biblical texts, and turn to a second general aspect of Barth's way of reading Scripture: *narrative exegesis.* Like the conceptual analysis of biblical texts, the narrative exegesis of biblical texts is a good candidate for consideration as a comprehensive designation of Barth's approach.[3] But is it? Is Barth a narrative expositor of Scripture? We shall return to this question in due course; for the present, however, it is important to become clear about just what features of Barth's exegesis one might aptly label "narrative exegesis." One soon finds, indeed, that there are several such features, to some extent overlapping, and yet likewise to some extent rather independent of one another.

There is first of all Barth's attempt to read the Bible as *saga*, or legend, as opposed to myth or history (cf. I.1, pp. 326-9). Reading the Bible as saga means realizing the unity of fact and value in biblical narration. It means denying to the Bible the category of myth (which sees narration of fact as the mere husk for presentation of value or meaning) or history (which falsely appropriates to the Bible the modern foundational concept of a "pure fact", to which values and meaning are only consequently, by interpretation, attached). For the most part Barth uses the concept of saga in expounding texts in Genesis and the Gospels. In a sense, it is a straightforwardly historical-critical category, unquestionably dependent upon the early development

---

[3] David Ford uses one version of the concept of narrative as the key to Barth's exegesis and theology as a whole. I have presented Ford's view, and a critical response to it, in the Introduction to this study.

of form-criticism (interestingly enough Gunkel and the Old Testament rather than Dibelius and the New).

A second feature, which overlaps with the first and yet is independent of it, is Barth's repeated attempts to distinguish biblical narrative from modern history with respect to the concept of *reference* (I.2, pp. 492-5). This is the central feature of Barth's exegesis for combatting historical criticism as a whole. Barth nowhere denies to the Bible reference in general; in fact his concept of witness actively endorses *attestation* of an object (see chapter one above). He always denies, however, that the object to which the biblical text points can be sought and investigated independently of its rendering in the biblical text. We have this object only in its biblical rendering; the historical-critical attempt to go *behind* the biblical text in search of a historical reality is *in principle* a confusion of categories in appropriating the form of the truth which the Bible offers us. Barth reads the Bible as narrative instead of history (or historical source), meaning that he systematically refuses to move beyond the text itself in meditating upon its object. This move is really a *literary* application of 'narrative' rather than a *historical* one like saga.

There is, thirdly, in Barth's exegesis what might be called a *narrative of revelation*. That is, Barth's overall concept of revelation has a strong temporal dimension. I am thinking here of the dialectic expectation-presence-recollection which occurs frequently in the biblical exegesis in these volumes. The movement from expectation to presence to recollection is the movement of the revelation of God in the Bible, from Old Testament (expectation) to the Incarnation (presence-- really the forty days between the resurrection and the ascension) to the New Testament witness (recollection). It is also the movement of revelation in the life-story of innumerable biblical characters, who move from expectation to recollection and back to fresh expectation, as well as the movement of revelation in the life-story of the reader of the Bible. Indeed, the echo of the general movement of the revelation of God in the Bible in the movement of revelation in the life-story of the individual reader is the closest thing in Barth to the narrative fusion of horizons.

A fourth aspect of Barth's exegesis of the Bible which should be characterized as narrative in approach is his tendency to read the Bible as attesting a God Who, in His very being, as well as in His relation to humanity, lives a life that can only be narrated. God Himself is history; God in His relation to us is history; indeed we know the internal history that God is on account of the external history with us that He enacts. And this history which God Himself is and enacts toward us is very often the "object" of the biblical text according to Barth's exegesis of it.[4]

A series of distinctions is used by Barth to carry out this particular aspect of his biblical exegesis. There is first of all the distinction between actuality and possibility. Biblical texts, according to Barth, uniformly follow the logical procedure: actuality of God's revealed Word, then possibility in God's sovereign Subject-hood. Because they move from actuality to possibility they must be read as narrative; any other reading would violate the internal *ratio* of this logical procedure, resulting in a misconstrual of their witness. Secondly, Barth employs the distinction between Being and Act. The biblical witness attests God's Being and God's Act, but only God's Being *in* God's Act. "God's Act" (or sometimes "Event" in the English) is one of the most

---

[4] David Kelsey, in his *The Uses of Scripture in Recent Theology* (Philadelphia: Fortress Press, 1975), pp. 39-50, has expertly described this particular dimension of Barth's narrative exegesis.

frequent phrases in Barth's biblical exegesis.   He will
often say of the biblical text that it "reports" or renders
an "account" of God's Act (of creation, of reconciliation,
of deliverance of Israel, of healing a man, of speaking to
a prophet, etc.).   A third distinction which Barth uses is
that between the scientific world of "being" and the
personal world of history.   According to Barth, the God
attested in Holy Scripture is rightly known by us in
analogy to the concept of historical agency rather than
in analogy to the concept of a natural fact.   Barth has
clearly appropriated here the German Idealists'
distinction between nature and history, reaffirming the
tradition that says that God is to be conceived under the
category of history rather than nature.   The result is,
again,   that   the biblical witness is conceived by Barth to
be such as is appropriate to the attesting of this history
(rather than the description of this factual condition).   It
is therefore to be read under the rubric of narrative.   So,
actuality and possibility, being and act, nature and
history; each of these distinctions is employed by Barth
to analyze what is at stake in reading the Bible as the
rendering of God's internal and external history, a
feature of what we are here calling narrative exegesis.

A fifth, and final feature of Barth's biblical exegesis
that can be characterized as narrative is the vast,
temporal sub-structure which he gives to the Bible as a
whole.   This internal structure is characterized by a
series of nodal points, nodal points which are *events* in
the common history of God and humanity as it is told
throughout the biblical text.   Any given individual
biblical text may not have anything to do with these
narrative nodal points;   it is often the case, however,
that such a text will be exegetically related by Barth to
one or more of these nodal points in the interpretation
of it.   The Bible as a whole both contains, and is contained
by, the nodal points of its narrative structure.

Now, just what are these nodal points? Strangely enough, no single answer can be given to this question. At times, it is as if there are only a few such structural pillars in the narrative world of the Bible; these are usually creation, reconciliation, and consummation, such that every biblical text is read in the light of one of these nodal points, or is given a setting in the repeated pattern of temporal dialectic which these engender throughout time. At other times, the temporal structure of the biblical world rests more on key moments in biblical history: the Garden of Eden, Noah, the calling of Abraham, the Exodus, the Monarchy, and so forth up through the resurrection, the forty days, the ascension, and the time of the church. The temporal structure of the biblical world is contributed by these key moments, and by the flow of time in the periods between them. Barth is indeed at times conscious of "periods" of biblical history; he nevertheless tends in his exegesis to concentrate on the nodal points which embrace a biblical period rather than the period of time itself. Here is no "dispensationalism", orthodox protestant or modern conservative; the nodal points which embrace a period are far more important than a precise description of the period itself, and even when Barth uses the concept of biblical periods (which is certainly not all the time) the nodal points are not so much like walls which separate the periods (the Adamic period, the Noahic Covenant, and the like) as they are like periodic dips of the oar which rush along the flow of revelation through time. Whether using these many nodal points, or whether the fewer nodal points mentioned above, Barth the expositor of Scripture sees the narrated structure of the biblical world as entirely *fluid*, both forwards and backwards. Without violating the structure as such, Barth can take a given text and travel forward with it, say to the final consummation of all things, or backwards with it to the faith of Abraham, or to the time before

Creation. There is a loose narrative structure to the biblical world, but there is a great deal of *freedom* exegetically in relating any individual text to this narrative world. The biblical text is not, that is to say, constituted by so many narrative *episodes* which only make sense as non-interchangeable moments in one unbroken and unbreakable narrative line. Barth just does not read the Bible this way.[5]

Now, we have presented five different aspects of Barth's biblical exegesis that might be considered narrative exegesis. Do they share anything in common? Do they interrelate together in such a way as to constitute a comprehensive narrative approach which explains each of them in turn? I cannot see that they do. I consider each of these five aspects as relatively independent of one another. I consider it a mistake to mention now one, now the other, as if they are all obviously manifestations of a single underlying theoretical approach. I furthermore consider it a mistake to single out any one of these five aspects as the one aspect that constitutes or explains Barth's "narrative approach". It seems, rather, far more accurate to argue that the *impetus* for any one of these narrative aspects is contributed either by a very

---

[5] A sixth narrative element could be added at this point, the one that Dr. Ford seizes on as the key to Barth's exegesis. Beginning with Barth's consideration of covenant-history in III.1, but emerging most clearly in the Christological sections of volume IV is a narrative exegesis which centers around the gospel story of Jesus Christ. In Dr. Ford's hands this type of exegesis becomes *the* characteristic of Barth's exegesis, and the one that is used to explain the biblical exegesis as a whole. Perhaps Dr. Ford is correct in making such a comprehensive ascription, though I question whether even there the narrative exegesis of the gospel story becomes anything more than a narrative element in Barth's exegesis, as opposed to the foundational exegetical method. At any rate, in the particular volumes under review here this exegetical move is less fully represented than the narrative elements we have considered above.

definite polemical context or by Barth's appropriation of a traditional Christian pattern of presentation rather than by a foundational, comprehensively explanatory narrative method, approach, or vision of the world. There are thus narrative elements in Barth's exegesis rather than a single narrative method. These elements can meaningfully and rightly be grouped together under the rubric of narrative exegesis because of a methodological concern on the part of the reader of the *Church Dogmatics*; to argue that these elements are grouped together so by Barth himself is misleading and unhelpful.

Let us now return to the main question of this part of our study. Does Barth do narrative exegesis of the Bible? Is Barth's approach best characterized as a narrative approach? We have above concluded that the narrative elements of Barth's exegesis do not constitute a narrative theory or the like. We now ask whether these elements are sufficiently notable to constitute a characteristic of Barth's exegesis prominent enough to be mentioned alongside of conceptual analysis as the best way to characterize Barth's exegesis as a whole. Granted that Barth does not employ a narrative theory in reading the Bible in various ways that might be called narrative exegesis; do the characteristically narrative elements in his reading of the biblical text really stand out above the many other characteristics of his biblical exegesis?

Against conceiving of Barth as doing narrative exegesis the following might be argued. Certain characteristics one customarily associates with the narrative reading of biblical texts are notably *absent* from Barth's biblical exegesis. The common narrative world shared by God as the primary Character, the biblical text itself, and the reader of the text is entirely lacking. Indeed, just the opposite is the case; the coming of Jesus Christ into the world, though it enters common narrated time, brings with it the *new aeon*, the new time, God's own time, which shatters and destroys what is now seen as the old aeon of the narrative world in which we live. But we *cannot narrate this new time* because it is concealed from us, though entirely real. Thus, neither the old aeon nor the new constitutes a stable narrative world; and Barth accordingly does not rely on or use such a narrative universe in the explication of biblical texts. Similarly, the God who is the major agent, the major character in a narrative reading of the Bible is presented by Barth as pre-temporal, supra-temporal, and post-temporal. That is, while the story of God's common history with humanity can be told, the relation which God has with His history with us violates the interrelation of plot, character, and circumstance in narrative reading. God creates, governs, enacts, possesses the narrative; God is the condition of the possibility of the narrative, rather than *vice versa*. We can trust the narrative rendering of God's history with us, *not* because that is all we have, but because with this narrative we have God's promise. Only God's promise stands between us and the possible dissolution of this narrative.

This lack of a unitary, stable narrative world is evidenced in Barth's exegesis by the lack of a systematic narrative reading of texts. There are times, indeed, when Barth will employ in his reading of a biblical text one or more of the narrative elements that we have described above; but there are likewise times when he will not, on occasions when the opportunity to do so is surely there. And there are even some occasions when a basically narrative text is expounded in such a way as to strip it of its characteristically narrative features. Nevertheless, having demurred in the strongest possible terms from the view that Barth employs a narrative theory of some sort in his reading of biblical texts, I do want to argue that narrative elements in his biblical exegesis are sufficiently noteworthy to constitute a characteristic rivalling conceptual analysis. Narrative elements are not foundational; they are however pervasive. It makes no sense to find a narrative theory in Barth (least of all a narrative aesthetic), but it likewise makes no sense to ignore the strong presence of narrative elements. *If* one had to give a systematic account for the narrative elements, the place to look would be, in my judgement, Barth's appropriation of traditional patterns of argument and presentation in Christian discourse from Augustine, to Calvin, to Cocceius, and so forth. However, I find missing in Barth, not only the attempt to articulate in theological exegesis a narrative theory or aesthetic of some sort, but likewise the attempt systematically to articulate an intramural Christian narrative theory of doctrine and exegesis. It just isn't there.

To recapitulate: two answers have now been given concerning the question of how to account for the movement from text to exegesis in Barth's explication of the biblical text. On the one hand is explication as conceptual analysis, and on the other hand is explication as narrative exegesis. Conceptual analysis of the biblical text proceeds through conceptual definition and conceptual clarification to the conceptual construal of the biblical text in relation to the key concepts of biblical, traditional Christian, and contemporary ecclesial language. Narrative exegesis, as detailed above, is not so much a unitary theory or method, as a collection of several approaches which have been linked together for our purposes under a single rubric. And yet while diverse in orientation and context, each of these elements shares something that we call "narrative, " and together they constitute a second characteristic of Barth's explication of the text, a second answer to the question concerning the movement from text to exegesis.

There remains to be considered only how these two approaches, conceptual analysis and narrative exegesis, are related to one another in Barth's explication of the text. The relation is indeed complex. To begin with, it should be pointed out that, while there are numerous exegetical excursuses of conceptual analysis showing little evidence of a narrative reading, there are not any examples of a narrative reading without conceptual analysis. That is, whenever Barth offers a narrative reading of a passage, he always makes clear at the outset as well as throughout the explication the particular conceptual definition he is trying to make. The bulk of an excursus may be narrative re-telling; even so, the function of the narrative reading is always conceptual analysis of some sort. There is no question but that narrative exegesis is thus ordered to conceptual analysis (when, of course, the latter is defined as above as the church's self-examination of its contemporary witness on the basis of explication of the biblical text). The many other functions that might be performed by narrative reading (aesthetic, say, or moral) are largely absent.

And yet, while ordered to conceptual analysis, there is likewise no question but that narrative exegesis is more than just an *instrument* for conceptual analysis. Precisely because the narrative elements of Barth's exegesis are so diverse, and occur in so many varying contexts, there is no part of Barth's biblical exegesis that is completely removed from a narrative reading. Without such narrative elements the exegesis would be entirely different, the conceptual analysis would necessarily be of an entirely different sort (perhaps with a foundational anthropological theory, or some such context--who knows?). Narrative exegesis is ordered to conceptual analysis; it is nevertheless a *sine qua non* for Barth's approach.   Narrative without concept would indeed be blind; but likewise would concept without narrative be empty.   The relation between concept and narrative is never allegory.   There is a sense, indeed, in which each functions as a corrective to the other.   That is to say, narrative exegesis often has the function of filling out conceptual content in such a way as to guard against the idle straying of a piece of conceptual analysis from the immediate concern of the biblical text itself.   On the other hand, conceptual analysis largely has the function of harnessing the narrative exegesis for the purposes of theological reflection.   Otherwise stated, narrative exegesis keeps conceptual analysis Christian, while conceptual analysis keeps narrative exegesis theological.   The coordination of the two approaches in Christian theological exegesis of biblical texts is Barth's way of offsetting the (perceived) theological dangers in using either in isolation.   Narrative exegesis in the absence of conceptual analysis becomes literary criticism, not *theological* exegesis; conceptual analysis without narrative exegesis becomes philosophical discourse, not theological *exegesis* of biblical texts.[6]

---

[6]The difference between Barth's conceptual, theological use of narrative exegesis and that of literary critical uses lies, in part, in the *work* that the narrative exegesis is called upon to perform.   A good contrast to Barth can be found in a recent essay by Paul Ricoeur on "Interpretative Narrative," (from *Recherches de Science Religieuse* 73 (1985, pp. 17-38).   Ricoeur's analysis of the passion narrative of Mark in terms of the "narrativization of the kerygma" can be compared favorably with what one might find in volume IV of the *Church Dogmatics*.   Nevertheless, though the narrative exegesis is in many respects similar, for Ricoeur the analytical exercise functions as part of the larger enterprise of coming to grips hermeneutically with the literary category of "interpretative narrative."   For Barth, on the other hand, the exercise functions as part of the larger enterprise of the conceptual-theological presentation and criticism of the church's

Both are necessary, though narrative is ordered to concept. Do the two, however, ever touch methodologically? We have isolated for analysis each in turn, and have now argued that the relation between the two is one of ordered coordination. But what do the two share in common such that they can be ordered together at all? The first and most important answer is simply that the two share in common the function that each performs in the larger enterprise of church theology. Concept and narrative also overlap, however, in a more exegetically identifiable way, in the form of the narrative *pattern*. Not always, but at times the narrative elements of an exegetical excursus are related to the conceptual concern of the whole by means of a narrative pattern, a particular feature of plot or character that corresponds with the conceptual point under discussion. A good example would be an excursus in II.2 (pp. 354-407) which in part is meant to support the doctrinal point that Christian election is always dipolar (including election and rejection in necessary relation to one another). The exegesis supporting this conceptual point is mostly narrative; in other words, in this instance the point is nowhere made by quoting and explicating biblical texts which make a similar point. Rather, the conceptual point is supported by finding in biblical narrative a series of paired characters mutually necessary to one another (as elect and rejected) in that there occurs in the biblical rendering of the characters a unity through the exchange of opposites. This narrative 'unity through the exchange of opposites' is a narrative pattern, recurrent over several biblical texts and contexts. The narrative pattern ('unity through the exchange of opposites') functions to unite together the

testimony to Jesus Christ. Moreover, a fuller comparison of Ricoeur and Barth would likewise show to what extent the differing conceptions of the function of narrative exegesis spill over into the narrative analysis itself, yielding some important differences at the analytical level.

narrative rendering of character on the one hand, and the conceptual concern of the excursus on the other.   But it should not be thought that a narrative pattern is always involved in the ordering of narrative and concept in Barth's exegesis.   It is in fact not particularly frequent; but it is a sign of the mutual necessity and mutual addressability of these two approaches.

Example D: Judas the Betrayer

For this fourth, and final, representative exegetical excursus it was necessary to choose for close analysis an excursus that can bear the weight of representing, to some extent, Barth's exegetical approach as a whole. Such indeed is Barth's exegesis of the "determination of the elect" in the form of a presentation of Judas in the Bible (II.2, pp. 458-506).[7]   It nicely represents the two approaches presented above, narrative exegesis and conceptual analysis, as well as the unconfused yet undivided relationship between the two.   The excursus indeed falls into two parts: the analysis of the character of Judas and the conceptual analysis of "handing-over" in the New Testament; we shall consider each in turn.

In the course of this exegetical excursus, Barth presents an extensive, multi-layered explication of the figure of Judas as he appears in the New Testament. The narrative mode of analysis and presentation is like several such exegetical studies throughout the *Church Dogmatics.*   Barth makes use of every scrap of text concerning Judas in the New Testament, and by fitting the pieces together like the parts of a puzzle comes up with a portrait of Judas, his character, his end, and his ultimate status before God.   The figure of Judas which emerges has a kind of independence from any one

---

[7]Ford comments on this excursus in *Barth and God's Story,* pp. 84-90.

gospel's rendering; differences among the gospels are related, as is customary with Barth, to the common subject-matter--in this case the figure of Judas--rather than to the peculiar shape and tendency (redactional or otherwise) of the individual gospel. The Judas that emerges is thus the Judas of the canonical gospel, not, or not only, the Judas of any individual gospel. We begin with Barth's presentation of Judas as a character in the text. The first thing to be said on this score is that the character of Judas in the New Testament is a mystery, a contradiction, a conflict of opposing movements that seem to point in opposite directions without ever meeting. The first such contradiction is that the character of Judas is at the same time an apostle and yet the betrayer of Jesus. According to Barth, Judas is, and always is, an apostle, one of the twelve. The apostleship of Judas is like an indelible characteristic; it cannot be lost, not only to the consideration of posterity, but also to the call of Jesus. Judas is an apostle of Jesus Christ, no less than Peter or John, and he is such to the very end--even in his betrayal. Judas is inside, not outside the kingdom of God. The textual basis for this aspect of Judas' character is the most sparse; everything that Barth says in praise of Judas' calling is on the basis of his appearance in the apostolic lists (pp. 459-60). On the other hand, what is clear from several texts according to Barth's citations is that Judas is the great betrayer of Jesus. A true apostle, and a vile betrayer; the contrast of opposites is here, as in many exegetical contexts in Barth, the foundation for the narrative analysis of character.

The mysterious duality in the character of Judas is likewise represented by the contrast between the paltriness of the act of sin which he committed and the heinousness of the result. The act itself of identifying Jesus to his accusers was a minor matter of convenience. Nevertheless, the act stands as the first link in a narrative chain of events which leads to the death of Jesus Christ on the cross. The consequence of the act seems so monstrously to outstrip the nature of the act itself, once again lending to the character of Judas a kind of mysterious quality.

The most comprehensive duality in the figure of Judas is simply that between the character as such and his destiny. His destiny is to betray Jesus, to hand him over to his death, to inaugurate the murder of God's only Son. Judas is the great sinner in the Bible. And yet this horrible destiny of Judas is so unrelated to his character as such; he is nowhere presented as evil, as capable of or the least motivated toward the kind of destiny he inherits. Indeed, that is the point; his destiny is a kind of inheritance, an acquired characteristic that is not in the least predictably related to his character or conduct. Judas the character steps into a *role* that is there before him, for which he does not have, nor does he need, any particular qualifications. Judas is at the same time a *character*, one of the twelve apostles who follow Jesus about as his disciples, and a *role*, the great Betrayer of God's Son. The figure of Judas as a whole emerges in the point of *contrast* between these two aspects. To be sure, Judas commits an evil act: he sells Jesus out, and thus shows that he considers Jesus a means to an end. He thus uses his discipleship rather than living by it. But, though evil, such conduct is not such as to explain Judas' role in the New Testament. The point of Barth's rendering of the figure of Judas is precisely that there is no fatal flaw; and in that sense Judas is wrongly cast as a tragic character.

We turn now to Barth's exegetical rendering of the biblical depiction of Judas' end (pp. 465-71). The texts which Barth uses are of course the accounts of Judas' death in Mt. 27 and Acts 1. It is interesting to what extent Barth relies on a kind of interiorizing reading of the character of Judas to make the point he wishes to make.   He firstly argues that Judas "only wanted" the first small step (handing Jesus over) and not the final result of his death.   Judas wanted to assert his own "independence" with respect to Jesus, but nothing more, and certainly nothing so horrible as came about. Secondly, argues Barth, Judas' repentance is genuine-- contrite, verbal, and restitutionary.   Judas was truly sorry.   How does Barth know this?   Of course no text can be cited, just as no text can be cited to support his analysis of Judas' true motives and interests in handing Jesus over.   So, Barth returns to his original construal of Judas as once and always a true apostle (because he is listed among the twelve in the gospels).   A true apostle cannot not repent genuinely; therefore Judas' repentance was genuine, evangelical repentance.

Nevertheless, because he has already rejected the offer of grace--by rejecting Jesus--the promise of grace does not extend to him.   Barth will go on to qualify this result in a rather confusing, contorted manner; nevertheless, he strongly asserts that the Bible unambiguously denies the promise of grace to a repentant Judas.   His repentance is a rejected repentance.   And for that reason Judas kills himself according to Matthew.   Barth acknowledges the divergent account of Acts I and attempts a harmony that can basically be characterized as psychological.   Acts speaks of Judas "bursting open," which Barth glosses like this: "Judas perished from within himself . . . His inmost being moves irresistible to this explosion of his whole existence.   The man who kills Jesus also kills himself, even though he may not technically be a suicide" (p. 471). Needless to say, this is a case of harmonizing two accounts by merging one (Acts) into the other (Matthew).

The mystery of the figure of Judas is thus perpetuated in the depiction of his end. His repentance was genuine; his death, like his life, was indelibly characterized by his apostolic call. And yet his repentance was not met by a corresponding offer of divine grace. Unlike other characters in the New Testament (Peter, the thief on the cross, etc.), repentance is here rejected.

Moreover, another aspect to the mystery of the figure of Judas begins to emerge in Barth's rendering of his death. Like any character, the figure of Judas is identified by narrative, the narrative of his conduct in the surrounding circumstances of his life. Judas is a character like this; and yet in telling the story of Judas, one is also identifying the story of someone else. Judas' character emerges as a representative character; and in this instance he represents the apostles (hence the church) and the Jews (all Israel). In Judas' acts, the apostles act; in Judas' acts Israel acts. Now, this mechanism--typological representation--is a not uncommon feature of Barth's exegesis of narrative. The characters rendered in biblical narrative almost always "mean" something beyond their biblical depiction for Barth; or rather, in Barth's reading the Bible renders its characters in such a way as to extend their significance beyond the immediate narrative context. However, in the case of Judas, this supra-narrative significance becomes so great as to rival Jesus' own. In Judas, the church and Israel sin. And more prominently, in Judas the church and Israel *die*; his death takes on the same scope of vicarious suffering as Christ's own. Indeed, though we shall return to clarify this question, one begins to wonder whether the character of Judas has become the *necessary complement* to the character of Jesus. At any rate, the mystery of the figure of Judas is extended in this direction too.

The character of Judas, while ambiguous, is nonetheless that of the betrayer of Jesus; the end of Judas, while of mysterious significance, is nonetheless altogether horrible and destitute. What then can be said about the ultimate *status* of Judas? Who is Judas the Betrayer *coram Deo*? Once again, Barth seizes on the presence of contrasts in the figure of Judas to answer this question. On the one hand, there is enormous pressure in the Bible and in tradition to answer this question with unqualified judgement against Judas. Judas, before God, is lost forever, the very prototype of those who flee headlong from the grace of God to their own eternal perdition. On the other hand, argues Barth, there are signs that the answer to this question is not so straightforward. There is first of all the sign that Judas seems to step into a role that could have been occupied by any of the other apostles. When Jesus states that one of the disciples would betray him, *all* of the disciples must ask: "Lord, is it I?" Says Barth, "The tension of this scene, emphasized by all the Evangelists, clearly arises from the fact that although it was actually this one disciple, any of the others might equally well have been the one" (p. 471). Or again, there is the ambiguity over who protested at the use of expensive oil for the annointing at Bethany; John assigns the disgruntlement to Judas, while Mark assigns it to "some" and Matthew simply and explicitly to "the disciples". Why is this? Barth argues: "The New Testament does actually give these varying accounts of the matter, and in so doing it says something which no reader of the New Testament Canon can any longer disguise from himself; that what Judas said on this occasion could have been said by others of Jesus' company; indeed, that it could have been said by His disciples as such, those who did not betray Him; or conversely, that what was actually said by some or all the disciples could also have been an utterance of Judas on this occasion" (p. 472). Judas, thus, does not

Explication of the Text 141

seem to be the necessary occupant of his own role, nor the necessary recipient of the curse that is attached to it. (Notice, once again, the canonical portrait that is painted using the four gospels, with the same precise attention to textual variation that is used by others to reconstruct literary history. The difference lies in the *aim* of exegesis, not in the attention to detail as such.)

And so, what is Judas' status *coram Deo*? Is he inside or outside the scope of God's grace and mercy? Does God forgive the sin of Judas? This question about Judas, just as it is for everyone else, is to be answered with reference to the death of Jesus Christ on the cross for the sins of many. Christ dies on the cross, taking the curse against humanity upon his shoulders, that he might extend, having been resurrected from the dead, His own blessedness to those who believe. Does this blessed exchange (of the curse of disobedience for the blessedness of obedience) apply to Judas as well? We have seen that, in Barth's opinion, there are signs in the New Testament that point in each direction in answer to this question, signs that the blessing of Christ passes Judas by, and signs that it must reach him too. And so, according to Barth, the question *must be left unanswered.* That is, the ultimate status of Judas *coram Deo* is, according to the New Testament, an open question. Judas exists in what Barth calls the "open situation of proclamation" (the idea is of course that of Lutheran doctrine). Both from the side of Jesus who addresses Judas with the promise, as well as from the side of Judas who responds, there is no final determination in the New Testament as to the outcome of this encounter.

Now two points should be made about this, Barth's elegant solution to the problem he has posed concerning Judas' status. First of all, Barth has introduced the "open situation of proclamation" to account for the inherent

open-endedness of the situation.   The general thrust of
the idea is clear enough, because it has a long legacy in
the history of Protestant doctrine; when asking
concerning one's election, so the doctrine goes, do not
look into the mysterious life of God from all eternity;
look rather to the offer of Christ in the proclamation of
the Word.   Here is ones election or rejection decided.
The idea is clear; but how is it referred by Barth to
Judas? Is Jesus preaching to Judas? Or someone else
preaching Christ to him? Is it during his life? If so,
when?   Is Barth referring indeed to an encounter
between Judas and Jesus at death? Or beyond death?
Barth introduces the "open situation of proclamation" to
account, with almost mathematical elegance, for the
contrasting signs on each side of the equation.   But he
nowhere gives even a clue as to what this situation
entails.

Secondly, it should be noticed that the solution which
Barth poses is inherently unstable from Barth's own
point of view.   Barth has placed every emphasis on
maintaining an *open* situation between Jesus and Judas.
And yet, anyone who has read a page of Barth's theology
will know that, when the grace of Jesus is juxtaposed
with the rebellion of humankind, there is *no doubt* as to
which way the balance will totter.   Jesus *never loses*
this encounter.   Jesus *always wins* this encounter.   Barth
has bet everything exegetically on keeping the question
of Judas' status *unanswered*, by leaving the question at
all costs an *open* one.   But the situation that Barth has
introduced to maintain this openendedness is the least
likely to guarantee an "open encounter."   Indeed, Barth
himself seems hardly able to refrain from taking back
with the left hand what he has just given with the right:
he speaks of the utter strength and irresistibility of the
grace of Christ, and the weakness of Judas' disobedience
in the face of it, concluding that, whether Judas may have

been converted or not, "this is how it always is in the situation of proclamation" (p. 477).

Having completed his presentation and analysis of the character of Judas, his end, and his ultimate status *coram Deo*, Barth then abruptly ends the narrative exegesis and turns instead to conceptual analysis (the German text has an actual break in the excursus). The biblical concept which he expounds is the concept of "handing-over"; as we shall see, in analyzing this concept he is in fact extending and deepening his portrayal of the figure of Judas. The concept of handing over has three natural settings in the new Testament according to Barth: Judas' betrayal of Jesus, the apostolic delivery of the gospel, and the divine handing-over of sinners into their own hands. Before turning to these three facets, it should be pointed out that the Greek word underlying "betrayal," "delivery," and "handing-over," is the same in each case (*"paradounai"*). To my knowledge, no other expositor, ancient or modern, has used this word and concept to make the exegetical points that Barth makes. Needless to say, the connections are really apparent only in Greek--neither the English nor the German have a single lexical item that matches the scope of the Greek word. Moreover, not only would a proficient knowledge of Greek (and a good Greek concordance) be necessary to read these texts the way Barth does, but so would the precise control that he has of the doctrinal issue under discussion and the way the texts address that issue. That is to say, Barth's reading is a technically brilliant achievement; and that is why it is all the more unfortunate that he has chosen such a poor rhetoric of persuasion to recommend it. Everything in Barth's reading is "obvious," "clear," or "impossible not to see"; it is as if Barth must convince his readers of the rightness and fit of his reading of these texts by convincing them that any intelligent or half-intelligent reader would come to the same conclusion he does. Barth has unfortunately replaced, against his own theological views and interests, perspicuity as the Bible's ability to shed light on its own meaning with perspicuity as the preference for only "obvious" readings. And because the readings Barth gives are anything but obvious, the persuasive power of his rhetoric is minimal.

At any rate, Barth analyzes the New Testament concept of handing-over in three contexts. The first is, of course, Judas' handing-over of Jesus to his enemies. The second is the apostolic handing-over of the gospel to future generations. Whereas the first meaning is predominantly *negative* (Judas' betrayal), the second is predominantly *positive* (the preaching of the gospel). The third meaning is the ultimate basis for the other two. It has both a negative and a positive side; on the one hand, God delivers sinners over to their eternal perdition when, in His wrath, he abandons them to their abandonment of Him. On the other hand, God executes this same delivery with reference to Jesus Christ, His only Son. God hands Jesus over, in His wrath, to eternal death, this time to the salvation of the world in Him. Thus God's delivery comprehends both a negative and a positive moment; the negative, however, is ultimately transposed into the positive.

What is the point? Firstly, the negative figure of Judas, by analysis of the concept of "handing-over," is seen to be a *paired* figure with the apostles, especially Paul. The pattern of Judas' conduct is the negative mirror image of the pattern of Paul's conduct. Moreover, both aspects of handing-over are comprehended in the divine handing-over as the Master Pattern. Like the conduct of Judas, God too hands sinners over to their evil fate; like Paul, God hands over His only Son to the ultimate salvation of the world. When viewed in the light of the divine handing-over, both the negative (Judas) and the positive (Paul) are seen to be *necessary* reflections in human conduct of the divine conduct. By analysis of the concept of handing-over Barth has thus extended his portrayal of the figure of Judas beyond the more obvious limits of his character in the New Testament into the broad reaches of the divine economy. Let us now summarize and conclude what we have to say about this exegetical excursus. The subject-matter for the excursus as a whole is the concept of the determination, the life-content, of the individual rejected person. What does the Christian confession have to say about those rejected in God's eyes? Biblical exegesis in answer to this question must concentrate, according to Barth, on the figure of Judas. Barth thus gives a narrative reading of the identity of Judas: his character, his end, and his status *coram Deo*. The narrative reading, however, does not yield an uncomplicated rendering; the final picture is in fact irresolute. The identity of Judas as it is told in the New Testament is a mysterious collision of opposites: a called apostle who is yet Christ's betrayer; a character in whom conduct and destiny never truly meet; a terrible sinner whose death seems to mirror Christ's own. The narrative reading of Judas is thus incomplete; and so Barth must extend and deepen his rendering of Judas by conceptual analysis of the concept of "betrayal" or "handing-over" as it is used in the New Testament. Analysis of this usage yields the surprising fact that Judas' negative act is a mirror-image of the apostolic act of proclaiming the gospel; and that, furthermore, the act of Judas and the act of the apostles are comprehended in the dual image of the handing-over of Jesus Christ for the sake of sinners. The pattern of Judas' conduct is thus merged with the pattern of Christ's own conduct; whatever must be said of Judas can only reflect the fact that, in the final analysis, his character is but a shadow cast backward by the character of Jesus Himself. Such is the yield of the conceptual analysis of "handing-over".

So what is the final picture of Judas? How do the narrative reading and the conceptual analysis fit together? The conceptual analysis in fact clarifies the mystery of the narrated identity of Judas. The conflict of character and destiny is now seen to be the result of the fact that Judas played a *role*, a *necessary* role, a role whose explanation lies not in the character of Judas at all but in the eternal plan of God. Because of who Jesus is, because of the salvation that God has willed from eternity past to enact in this man, the work that He does *must necessarily* cast a shadow around him in the form of a betrayer who must hand him over. Judas is chosen as this betrayer. This is indeed his rejection. To be rejected means to play the role of the one who hands Christ over. His rejection is then the *role* that he plays, *not* an inherent characteristic of his character or conduct. The mystery of the figure of Judas is that the rejected role that he must necessarily play is unpredictably related to the character that he is as such.

Rejection is thus a role willed by God. Judas is *elected* to rejection. The only remaining question is whether the narrative ever catches up with the fact that Judas is inside, not outside, the electing will of God. That is, does the story of Judas ever manifest the fact that his role is as the rejected chosen by God to be such? Barth's first answer to this question is to speak of the "open situation of proclamation," to insist, therefore, that the question be purposefully unanswered. Whether Judas will thus embrace the election in his rejection is to be left open. As he continues, however, Barth begins to mention the "eschatalogical possibility of salvation", referring apparently to a continuation of Judas' story into the future beyond death at a point when the elected nature of his rejected role will be manifest (pp. 476-7). Somewhat like Kant's argument for the immortality of the soul, Barth extrapolates beyond death the story of Judas, projecting forward a new encounter with the proclaimed grace of Jesus Christ, as a way of accounting for the discrepancy between his role (rejection) and the ultimate origin of that role in the will of God. The conceptual analysis not only clarifies and explains the narrative reading; in this instance it generates it anew.

Chapter 5

Conclusion

What, then, can be said about Karl Barth's biblical exegesis in the first two volumes of the *Church Dogmatics*? We conclude, now, with a summary and evaluation of the results of this study.

In Chapter 1 it was argued that the most comprehensive answer to the question concerning the nature and substance of Barth's biblical exegesis is a statement concerning the *function* of the biblical text in Barth's exegesis of it. The concept of *witness* was used to describe that function. That the biblical text functions as a witness to divine revelation is the foundation of the description of Barth's exegesis. Indeed, the concept of witness answers the question of whether the pluralism of Barth's biblical exegesis--the lack, that is, of a systematic hermeneutic in its support, and the irreducibly pluralistic form of its procedures and problems--leads ultimately to incoherence. It is in fact the basic *function* of the biblical text in Barth's exegesis of it that renders the seemingly chaotic variety of Barth's exegesis a coherent whole.

The function of witness is divided into two aspects: the content of the Bible as a *text*, and the object of the Bible in the divine *Word*. In the analysis of the concept of the Bible's textuality it was argued that the final form of the biblical text receives Barth's exegetical attention; but not just the final form *per se*, but the final form as the textual rendering of one or more "themes" which in turn serve to attest the object of the biblical witness. The point of departure for locating the witness of the text is in the text itself; it is not a second level of exegesis simply added on to the first. This thematic point of departure in the text is usually on the surface level of the content of the text, though it may also be concealed behind the surface or only implied in it; nevertheless, it is always there, whether present, concealed, or implied.

The concept of witness entails a textual content; it likewise entails the exegetical search for the *object* of the biblical text. The movement from text to object is a logical circle; we have the object only in its textual rendering, and yet only the knowledge of this object provides the condition for the possibility of true exegesis of the text. Indeed, it is the problematic relation between text and object which constitutes the driving force of all biblical exegesis for Barth; it is the true enactment of this relation in the exegesis of the biblical text which corresponds to the proper function of the Bible: bearing witness.

The relation between text and object consists of *analogical depiction*. The depiction of an object highlights the direct, immediate aspect of biblical witness for Barth. The concept of analogy, on the other hand, highlights the more problematic, indirect, mediate aspect. Nevertheless, it is the *reader* who becomes problematic in analogical reading, not the text or its object *per se*. Analogy does not describe an exegetical procedure in which the content of the text is interpreted in such a way as to yield a meaningful object to the reader; it rather describes a procedure in which the content of the text is used to interpret the world of the reader in such a way as to bring the reader face to face with the object of the biblical text. The flow of interpretation is thus from text to reader, rather than from reader (as presupposed, foundational world of meaning) to text.

Chapter 2 extended the analysis more particularly of the object of the biblical witness, by raising the issue of the Christological form and focus of much of Barth's exegesis. The issue of Christocentrism in exegesis is to be sharply distinguished from the relation between the Old and New Testaments. That is, one cannot account for the Christological direction of exegesis by appeal to the problematic status of the Old Testament, and this because the New Testament is equally problematic with respect to Jesus Christ as is the Old. Barth does not, in his exegesis, make use of any causal, historical relation that might be thought to subsist between the New Testament writings and the figure of Jesus Christ; the New Testament is as Christologically problematic as the Old.

Barth evidently tends toward some Christological reference in his presentation of the object of the witness of any given biblical text. This reference can occur, however, in two very different ways. On the one hand, the biblical text can be referred to Jesus Christ in the sense that Christological *concepts* can clarify or solve a conceptual problem in the text. On the other hand, Jesus Christ can be brought into relation to a biblical text in the form of the exegetical association of two or more narratives. In this latter instance-- classically referred to as typology--the narrated person of Jesus Christ functions as the overarching narrative context into which individual biblical narratives are placed for their interpretation.

Corresponding to the twofold distinction in the way Jesus Christ is brought into relation to a biblical text is a distinction between two very different subjects so related. On the one hand is the *logical* subject Jesus Christ, the logical subject, that is, of what Barth calls the "predicates" of the biblical witness. That is to say, in this instance Jesus Christ is represented by Barth as the logical possessor of all the theological values in the Bible, both positive and negative. The identity of this logical subject emerges as the center of these values. On the other hand, Jesus Christ can be presented by Barth as the narrated, personal subject of biblical stories. Here it is the Jesus Christ narrated in the gospels who becomes the object, the interpretive key for biblical texts. Biblical stories in this instance are given their interpretive context by exegetical association with a narrated subject, whose identity is already certain and well-defined as he comes to these stories.

The close analysis of the exegesis of the story of the Rich Young Ruler yielded the further insight that Christocentric exegesis can indeed move a narrative biblical text *away from* a narrative reading. That is to say, the impulse toward a Christological reading is not only not equivalent to, or necessarily accompanied by, an impulse toward a narrative reading; on occasion at least a Christological reading can in fact override and cancel out the narrative reading of a narrative text.

In chapter 3 the study expanded its analysis of Barth's biblical exegesis to include the conceptual and theological *context* in which it is conducted. There are evidences in Barth's exegesis of pressures exerted upon the exegesis by Barth's theological views and interests. Chief among these signs of the presence of Barth's theological concerns in Barth's biblical exegesis is the pervasive attempt on Barth's part to expound the Bible in terms of the *concepts* it yields. The search for biblical concepts is a sign of a theological presence because the concept, as the fundamental unit of meaningful Christian discourse, is shared by biblical language, the language of Christian proclamation, and technical theological language. Thus, by expounding the Bible in terms of concepts Barth is able to insure the mutual fit of Bible, Church mission, and scientific theology.

A second sign of theological pressure on the biblical exegesis is the presence in the exegesis of formal patterns of argument that are dialectical, and which thus echo broader material positions which Barth elsewhere articulates in the main body of the dogmatic exposition. Veiled, unveiled; analytic, synthetic; subject, predicate; such are widespread patterns of exegetical argument and presentation that render the biblical text such that it corresponds to similar patterns of argument and presentation in the theological discourse proper.

A final sign of the presence in the exegesis of pressure from the theology is the high level of doctrinal precision in the biblical exegesis. That is to say, the Bible, in Barth's hands, is made to yield answers to questions of such doctrinal technicality and sophistication that, whatever the content of the answer, the sheer fact that an answer is yielded by biblical exegesis is a noteworthy characteristic of Barth's approach.

Along with the evidence of pressure from the theological discourse on the biblical exegesis there is likewise evidence of pressure from two other sources: traditional Christian theological language, and Barth's reading of other biblical texts (parallel passages). Each of these is a true presupposition: a condition for the possibility of the kind of exegesis Barth does. There is pervasive throughout Barth's exegesis an assumption of the mutual addressability of the biblical text and traditional Christian language, the mutual fit of their religious and theological concerns (even if at times antithetical). There is likewise pervasive throughout Barth's biblical exegesis an assumption of the mutual addressability of various biblical texts. The reading of one biblical text can be immediately and genuinely illuminated, whether critically and correctively or by corroboration and clarification, by the reading of another biblical text. The relation between the texts is formulated by Barth always in precise, disciplined exegetical strategies, though non-historical ones. In the final chapter, attention was turned to an accounting of the movement from text to exegesis in Barth's work. Barth's explication of the biblical text-- our version of Barth's exegetical *method*--is irreducibly twofold in character. There is firstly Barth's conceptual-analytical approach in the exegesis of biblical texts. Exegesis as the definition and clarification of biblical and theological concepts has a natural setting in Barth's work because of his particular conception of the "stuff" of dogmatics and exegesis that emerges from the proclamation of the Christian church. Conceptual analysis of biblical texts is an attempt to render Scripture in such a way that it addresses the task of the church in its theological self-examination. The relation of an individual concept and its analysis to this task, and to the question of truth ingredient in it, outweighs by far the question of the intrinsic, ontological status of concepts as such.

Barth's biblical exegesis is likewise to be characterized as narrative exegesis. At least five elements can be so characterized: Barth's use of the historical category of saga (as opposed to myth), his use of the literary category of story (as opposed to history), the pervasive presence of a narrative of revelation (expectation, presence, recollection), the internal and external history of God, and the narrative sub-structure of the Bible as a whole. While rightfully characterized as narrative elements, the attempt systematically to conceptualize these elements in the form of a foundational narrative hermeneutics should be resisted. To paraphrase Barth, narrative can become a predicate of revelation; but revelation is not a predicate of narrative.

Both narrative exegesis and conceptual analysis are necessary as exegetical approaches to biblical texts for Barth. Neither, in my judgement, is reducible to the other. However, as descriptions of Barth's exegetical procedure, it seems clear that narrative is ordered toward the conceptual analysis of texts. Because of its setting in the task of dogmatics and exegesis as a whole, conceptual analysis of biblical texts guides, at every turn, the narrative elements. While not underestimating the great importance of narrative exegesis, it is thus best to speak of a *broken narrative* reading of texts, rather than a consistent narrative reading.

Our analysis and presentation of Barth's biblical exegesis is now concluded. What the future holds for this corpus of biblical exegesis in relation to the coming agenda for theological exegesis, who can say? At the present, it certainly seems that the historical-critical study of the Bible in biblical studies on the one side, and the pursuit of theological hermeneutics (including those oriented to literary studies) in theology on the other, are unable to account for or absorb Barth's biblical exegesis. Barth's approach is simply not oriented to the historical-critical approach as it is professionally practiced; attempts to square his theological exegesis with the historical approach, or attempts to add remnants of Barth's approach on to the standard historical approaches, seem not to have really faced the challenge to biblical exegesis that Barth's work represents. Similarly, attempts to convert Barth's biblical exegesis into a theological hermeneutic (narrative or otherwise) -- whether or not this hermeneutic is used to generate exegesis anew--seem uniformly to strip the biblical exegesis of those very features which make it so worthy of study in the first place.   If Barth's biblical exegesis has a future in theological exegesis, it will in part be because it *expects* a future; that is to say, there is ingredient in Barth's biblical exegesis a *corrigibility* of exegesis with respect to the biblical text that predicts its own future transformation into fresh theological exegesis. When and if there comes a renewed attempt at the theological exegesis of biblical texts, an encounter with Holy Scripture beyond historical criticism and hermeneutics, Barth's biblical exegesis will surely be there, ready to hand.

Bibliography of Works Consulted

Alter, Robert. *The Art of Biblical Narrative.* New York, 1981.

Balthasar, Hans Urs von. *The Theology of Karl Barth.* New York, 1971.

Barr, James. *The Bible in the Modern World.* New York, 1973.

_____. *T he Semantics of Biblical Language.* Oxford, 1961.

_____. *Old and New in Interpretation.* London, 1966.

Barth, Karl. *Church Dogmatics I.1-IV.4.* Edinburgh, 1936-75.

_____. *Die Kirchliche Dogmatik I.1-IV.4.* and *Registerband.* Zurich, 1938-70.

_____. *The Epistle to the Romans.* London, 1933.

_____. *A Shorter Commentary on Romans.* Richmond, 1959.

Berkouwer, G. C. *The Triumph of Grace in the Theology of Karl Barth.* Grand Rapids, 1956.

Bromiley, Geoffrey W. *Introduction to the Theology of Karl Barth.* Grand Rapids 1979.

Bultmann, Rudolf. *Theology of the New Testament.* New York, 1955.

Busch, Eberhard. *Karl Barth.* Philadelphia, 1976.

Childs, Brevard S. *Biblical Theology in Crisis.* Philadelphia, 1972.

_____. *Introduction to the Old Testament as Scripture.* Philadelphia, 1979.

_____. *The New Testament as Canon: An Introduction.* London, 1984.

_____. *Old Testament Theology in a Canonical Context.* Philadephia, 1985.

_____. "The Sensus Literalis of Scripture: An Ancient and Modern Problem" in *Beitraege zur alttestamentlichen Theologie: Festschrift fuer Walther Zimmerli zum 70. Geburtstag.* ed. Herbert Donner et al., pp. 80-93. Goettingen, 1977.

Eichholz, G. "Der Ansatz Karl Barths in der Hermeneutik" in *Antwort*, pp. 52-68. Zurich, 1956.

Ford, David. *Barth and God's Story.* Frankfurt am Main, 1981.

_____. "Barth's Interpretation of the Bible" in *Karl Barth, Studies of His Theological Method .* ed. S. W. Sykes, pp. 55-87. London, 1979.

Frei, Hans W. *The Eclipse of Biblical Narrative.* New Haven and London, 1974.

_____. *The Identity of Jesus Christ.* Philadelphia, 1975.

_____. *The Doctrine of Revelation in the Thought of Karl Barth, 1909-1922.* Unpublished Yale Dissertation, 1956.

_____. "Eberhard Busch's Biography of Karl Barth" in *Karl Barth in Re-View*, ed. H. Martin Rumsheidt, pp. 95-116. Pittsburgh, 1981.

_____. "The 'Literal Reading' of the Biblical Narrative in the Christian Tradition: Does it Stretch or Will it Break?" in *The Bible and the Narrative Tradition*, ed. Frank McConnell, pp. 36-77. New York and Oxford, 1986.

Hartwell, Herbert. *The Theology of Karl Barth: An Introduction.* London, 1964.

Juengel, Eberhard. *Barth Studien.* Zurich, 1982.

Kelsey, David H. *The Uses of Scripture in Recent Theology.* Philadelphia, 1975.

_____. "The Bible and Christian Theology," *Journal of the American Academy of Religion*, XLVIII/3, pp. 385-402.

Klopfenstein, Martin A. "I Koenige 13" in *Parrhesia*, pp. 639-72. Zurich, 1966.

Konrad, J. F. *Abbild und Ziel der Schoepfung.* Tuebingen, 1962.

Kraus, Hans Joachim. *Die Biblische Theologie.* Neukirchen-Vluyn, 1970.

_____. *Geschichte der historisch-kritischen Erforschung des Alten Testaments.* Neukirchen-Vluyn, 1969.

_____. Vorwort to *Exegese von I Koenige 13* von Karl Barth. Breklum, 1955.

Kreck, Walter. *Grundentscheidungen in Karl Barths Dogmatik.* Neukirchen-Bluyn, 1978.

Kueng, Hans. *Justification: The Doctrine of Karl Barth and a Catholic Reflection.* New York, 1964.

Lindbeck, George A. *The Nature of Doctrine.* Philadelphia, 1984.

Lindemann, W. *Karl Barth und die kritische Schriftauslegung.* Hamburg-Bergstadt, 1973.

Marquardt, Friedrich Wilhelm. "Exegese und Dogmatik in Karl Barths Theologie" in Registerband to *Die Kirchliche Dogmatik* of Karl Barth, pp. 651-76. Zurich, 1970.

Preuss, James Samuel. *From Shadow to Promise.* Cambridge, 1969.

Ramm, Bernard. *After Fundamentalism.* San Francisco, 1983.

Ricoeur, Paul. "Interpretative Narrative," trans. David Pellauer, from article in *Recherches de Science Religieuse.* 73 (1985), pp. 17-38.

Runia, K. *Karl Barth's Doctrine of Holy Scripture.* Grand Rapids, 1962.

Schlichting, W. *Biblische Denkform in der Dogmatik.* Zurich, 1971.

Smend, Rudolf, "Nachkritische Schriftauslegung" in *Parrhesia,* pp. 215-37. Zurich, 1966.

Thiselton, Anthony. *The Two Horizons.* Grand Rapids, 1980.

Torrance, T. F. *Karl Barth: An Introduction to His Early Theology 1910-1931*. London, 1962.

Wharton, James A. "Karl Barth as Exegete and His Influence on Biblical Interpretation," *Union Seminary Quarterly Review*. Fall, 1972, pp. 5-13.

Wood, Charles M. *The Formation of Christian Understanding*. Philadelphia, 1981.